STREET SPANISH 3

Strictly for
Survival

To order the accompanying cassette for

STREET SPANISH 3

See the coupon on the last page for details

STREET SPANISH 3
The Best of Naughty Spanish

David Burke

John Wiley & Sons, Inc.

New York • Chichester • Weinheim • Brisbane • Singapore • Toronto

Design and Production: David Burke
Copy Editor: Alfonso Moreno-Santa
Front Cover Illustration: Ty Semaka
Inside Illustrations: Ty Semaka

This book is printed on acid-free paper. ∞

This publication is designed to provide accurate and authoritative
information in regard to the subject matter covered. It is sold with the
understanding that the publisher is not engaged in rendering professional
services. If professional advice or other expert assistance is required, the
services of a competent professional person should be sought.

Library of Congress Cataloging-in-Publication Data
Burke, David
    Street Spanish 3 : the best of naughty Spanish / David Burke.
      p. cm.
    Includes glossary.
    ISBN 0-471-17972-8 (pbk. : alk. paper)
    1. Spanish language - Slang.   2. Spanish language - Obscene words.
3. Invective.   4. Spanish language - Textbooks for foreign speakers -
English.   I. Title.
PC4961.B873   1998
467'.09 - dc21   98-12974

Printed in the United States of America
10 9 8 7 6 5 4 3

This book is dedicated to Chellie Powell...a total *pichón*!
[**pichón** *n.* beautiful girl, "hot chick" • (lit.): small bird]

ACKNOWLEDGMENTS

Once again, I'm forever grateful to Alfonso Moreno-Santa˙ for his extraordinary contribution to this book. His organization, eye for detail, creative flair, and insight into the spoken Spanish language were essential in the creation of this book. He will always have my deepest appreciation and regard.

To say that Ty Semaka's illustrations are brilliant, hilarious, amazing, and magical would be an understatement. I consider myself so lucky to have found such talent all wrapped up in one person.

My special thanks and most sincere admiration go to Chris Jackson, my editor at John Wiley & Sons. To date, I don't believe there has been a word or an idiom created which describes someone who is as professional, reassuring, attentive, enthusiastic, motivated, and fun as Chris. He made the entire process truly enjoyable.

I must give an enormous thanks to Diane, who is nothing less than amazing. It was an absolute pleasure to work with someone as masterful, thorough, adept, and affable as Diane.

CONTENTS

INTRODUCTION

You may be asking yourself, "What purpose could a book about Spanish obscenities possibly serve other than simply to create shock value by listing gratuitous vulgar words and expressions?" There are three simple answers: (1) to avoid embarrassment; (2) to understand fully a conversation between native speakers; and (3) survival.

Although many teachers prefer not to acknowledge this fact, obscenities are a living part of everyday Spanish. They are used in movies, books, television and radio shows, newspapers, news broadcasts, magazines, to name a few categories.

Those who are not completely familiar with the Spanish language often find themselves in awkward or embarrassing situations by using a word in such a way as to create a double meaning or a sexual innuendo. When I was visiting Argentina, an American friend of mine walked up to a police officer and very innocently asked him where he could catch the bus:

*¿Dónde puedo **coger** el autobús?*

What he meant to say was:

*¿Dónde puedo **tomar** el autobús?*

Not having a firm grasp on popular Spanish obscenities, he was quite unaware that he had just made a serious yet entertaining faux pas, since **coger** does *not* mean "to catch" in Argentina as it does in many other Spanish-speaking countries. In Argentina, it has one very specific meaning: "to fuck."

STREET SPANISH 3 is the first step-by-step guide of its kind to explore the most common expletives and obscenities used in Spanish. This knowledge is an essential tool in self-defense for nonnative speakers as well as an entertaining guide for native speakers who may not be aware of how colorful the Spanish language truly is.

STREET SPANISH 3 is a self-teaching guide made up of ten chapters, each divided into three primary parts:

■ DIALOGUE

Popular Spanish terms and idioms are presented as they may be heard in an actual conversation. A translation of the dialogue in standard English is always given on the opposite page.

■ VOCABULARY

This section spotlights all of the slang terms that were used in the dialogue and offers:

1. An example of usage for each entry;

2. An English translation of the example;

3. Synonyms, antonyms, variations, or special notes to give the reader a complete sense of the word or expression.

■ A CLOSER LOOK SECTION

This section introduces common idioms and slang pertaining to a specific category such as *vulgar insults and name-calling* and *body parts in slang*.

Whether you're a native Spanish-speaker or a visitor, **STREET SPANISH 3** will prove to be an essential yet hilarious guide to the darker and more colorful side of one of the world's most popular languages.

David Burke

Legend

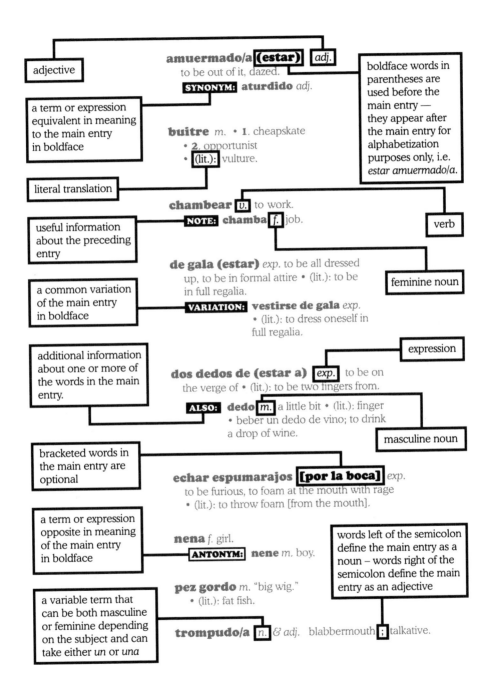

adjective

amuermado/a (estar) *adj.*
to be out of it, dazed.
SYNONYM: **aturdido** *adj.*

a term or expression
equivalent in meaning
to the main entry
in boldface

boldface words in
parentheses are
used before the
main entry —
they appear after
the main entry for
alphabetization
purposes only, i.e.
estar amuermado/a.

buitre *m.* • **1.** cheapskate
• **2.** opportunist
• (lit.): vulture.

literal translation

chambear *v.* to work.
NOTE: **chamba** *f.* job.

verb

useful information
about the preceding
entry

feminine noun

de gala (estar) *exp.* to be all dressed
up, to be in formal attire • (lit.): to be
in full regalia.
VARIATION: **vestirse de gala** *exp.*
• (lit.): to dress oneself in
full regalia.

a common variation
of the main entry
in boldface

expression

additional information
about one or more of
the words in the main
entry.

dos dedos de (estar a) *exp.* to be on
the verge of • (lit.): to be two fingers from.
ALSO: **dedo** *m.* a little bit • (lit.): finger
• beber un dedo de vino; to drink
a drop of wine.

masculine noun

bracketed words in
the main entry are
optional

echar espumarajos [por la boca] *exp.*
to be furious, to foam at the mouth with rage
• (lit.): to throw foam [from the mouth].

a term or expression
opposite in meaning
of the main entry
in boldface

nena *f.* girl.
ANTONYM: **nene** *m.* boy.

words left of the semicolon
define the main entry as a
noun – words right of the
semicolon define the main
entry as an adjective

pez gordo *m.* "big wig."
• (lit.): fat fish.

a variable term that
can be both masculine
or feminine depending
on the subject and can
take either *un* or *una*

trompudo/a *n. & adj.* blabbermouth ; talkative.

STREET SPANISH 3

The Best of Naughty Spanish

Alfonso *echa los perros* cuando ve a una *chava bien.*

(trans.): Alfonso **flirts** when he sees a **pretty girl**.
(lit.): Alfonso **throws dogs** when he sees a **well young girl**.

Carmen: ¡No lo puedo creer! Alfonso, el **cuero** que conocí la semana pasada, me **dejó plantada**. ¡Vaya! Otro **patán**.

Pilar: ¡Hombre! A todos los hombres les gusta **hacer ojitos**. Todos son **aficionados a las faldas** y muchos de ellos son **enfermos sexuales**. Siempre que ven a una **chava bien**, le **echan los perros** y piensan que ella es una **presa fácil**. Pero en cuanto piensan que quieres **atar el nudo**, te **dejan clavada**.

Carmen: ¡Oye! No solo son los hombres. Mi hermana es así también. La semana pasada **salió** con un **viejo rabo verde**. Si quieres saber mi opinión, a él le deben de **gustar los bebés** porque mi hermana todavía **huele a pañales**. Solo tiene 18 años. En cualquier caso, fue **amor a primera vista**. Pero en cuanto él mencionó que quiere **una boda por todo lo alto**, ella lo **dejó plantado**.

Pilar: ¿Por qué es tan difícil el amor algunas veces? Bueno, al próximo tipo que me **eche los perros** le voy a decir que mejor **se largue** y se vaya al cine a ver una **película equis**.

Alfonso flirts when he sees a pretty girl.

Carmen: I can't believe this! Alfonso, the **hunk** that I met last week, **stood me up**. Oh, brother! Another **jerk**.

Pilar: Men! They all like to **flirt**. They're all **playboys** and many of them have **sex on the brain**. Every time they see a **hot chick**, they **try to pick her up** assuming that she's an **easy lay**. But as soon as they think you want to **tie the knot**, they **dump** you.

Carmen: Listen! It's not just guys. My sister is like that, too. Last week, she **went out** with a **dirty old man**. If you ask me, he must **like to rob the cradle** because my sister still **looks like a baby**. She's only 18 years old. In any case, it was **love at first sight**. But as soon as he mentioned that someday he wants to **have a big wedding**, she **dumped him**.

Pilar: Why is love so hard sometimes? Well, the next guy who starts to **flirt with** me, I'm going to tell him **to scram** and go to the movies and see a **dirty movie** instead.

Vocabulary

aficionado a las faldas *exp.* to be a playboy, to be a skirt-chaser • (lit.): to be a fan of the skirts.

example:
Luis es muy **aficionado a las faldas**. Todas la noches sale con una mujer diferente.

translation:
Luis is a real **playboy**. He goes out with a different woman every night.

NOTE: The English term "playboy" is also widely used among Spanish-speaking people.

SYNONYM -1: detras de las faldas (estar) *exp.* • (lit.): to be behind the skirts.

SYNONYM -2: mujeriego (ser) *n. & adj.* playboy; womanizing.

amor a primera vista *exp.* love at first sight • (lit.): [same].

example:
Lo de Alvaro y Fiona fue **amor a primera vista**.

translation:
For Alvaro and Fiona, it was **love at first site**.

ALSO: enamorarse de un flechazo *exp.* to fall in love with someone all of a sudden • (lit.): to become enamored as a result of a wound from a love-arrow.

atar el nudo *exp.* to get married • (lit.): to tie the knot.

example:
¿Has oído la noticia? ¡Angel va a **atar el nudo** la semana que viene!

translation:
Did you hear the news? Angel is going **to get married** next week!

chava bien *f. (Mexico)* hot chick • (lit.): well young girl.

example:
Monica es una **buenona**. Me gustaría mucho salir con ella.

translation:
Monica is a **hot chick**. I would love to go out with her.

> **VARIATION:** **chava bien buena** *f. (Mexico)* extremely hot and sexy girl.
>
> > **NOTE:** **chavo bien** *m. (Mexico)* hot guy • (lit.): well young guy / **chavo bien bueno** *m.* extremely hot and sexy guy.
>
> **SYNONYM -1:** **bombón** *m.* • (lit.): bonbon (a type of chocolate candy).
>
> **SYNONYM -2:** **buenona** *f. (Spain)* • (lit.): very good.
>
> **SYNONYM -3:** **caramelo** *m. (Spain)* • (lit.): caramel candy.
>
> **SYNONYM -4:** **merengue** *f. (Spain)* • This is a type of sweet cake.

cuero *m.* hunk, "hot guy" • (lit.): leather.

example -1:
Juan es un verdadero **cuero**. Todas las mujeres quieren salir con él.

translation:
Juan is a real **hunk**. Every woman wants to go out with him.

> **SYNONYM:** **chulo/a** *adj. (Spain)* • **1.** hunk • **2.** cool person or object • (lit.): pimp.
>
> > **NOTE:** The term *chulo* is so popular among Spanish-speaking people, that is has even been transformed into the verb *chulear* meaning "to act cool."
> >
> > **ALSO:** **chulear de** *exp.* **1.** to brag about [something] • **2.** to show off.
> >
> > example -1:
> > Roberto **chulea de** ser un experto.
> >
> > translation:
> > Roberto **brags about** being an expert.

example -2:
A Luis le gusta **chulear su** casa.

translation:
Luis loves **to show off** his house.

dejar clavado/a a alguien *exp.* • **1.** to dump someone • **2.** to be stood up • (lit.): to leave someone nailed.

example -1:
¡Marcelo **me dejó clavada** por otra chica!

translation:
Marcelo **dumped me** for another girl!

example -2:
Marta **me dejó clavado**. Nunca se presentó a nuestra cita.

translation:
Marta **stood me up**. She never showed up for our date.

dejar plantado/a a alguien *exp.* • **1.** to dump someone • **2.** to be stood up • (lit.): to leave someone planted.

example:
Ayer tenía una cita con Carmen pero **me dejó plantado**.

translation:
I had a date with Carmen yesterday, but she **stood me up**.

echar los perros *exp.* to flirt, to try to pick someone up • (lit.): to throw dogs.

example:
Los albañiles tienen fama de **echarle los perros** a cualquier mujer que pasa delante de ellos.

translation:
Construction workers are known for **flirting** with any woman that passes by.

SYNONYM -1: **hacer ojitos** *exp.* • (lit.): to make little eyes.

SYNONYM -2: **lanzarse** *v.* • (lit.): to go for it.

enfermo sexual *exp.* sex pervert, to have sex in the brain • (lit.): sexually sick.

  example:
  Ernesto es un verdadero **enfermo sexual**. No piensa en otra cosa.

  translation:
  Ernesto is a real **sex pervert**. That's all he thinks about.

  SYNONYM: siempre caliente (estar) *exp.* to be sexually excited all the time • (lit.): to be hot (or "in heat") all the time.

gustar los bebés *exp.* to rob the cradle • (lit.): to like babies.

  example:
  A José le **gustan los bebés**. Siempre sale con niñas muy jóvenes.

  translation:
  Jose likes **to rob the cradle**. He always goes out with very young girls.

hacer ojitos *exp.* to lead someone on, to flirt • (lit.): to make little eyes.

  example:
  Jorge le estaba **haciendo ojitos** a Ana en la fiesta.

  translation:
  Jorge was **flirting** with Ana at the party.

largarse *exp.* to scram, to leave in a hurry, to go away, to split. • (lit.): to let go.

  example:
  En cuanto Luis escuchó la noticia de que su esposa estaba a punto de dar a luz, ¡**se largó**!

  translation:
  As soon as Luis got the news that his wife was about to give birth, **he left in a hurry**!

  SYNONYM: desaparecer *v.* • (lit.): to disappear.

oler a pañales *exp.* to look like a baby, to be very young • (lit.): to smell like diapers.

> example:
> ¿Adriana es médico? ¡Pero si todavía **huele a pañales**!
>
> translation:
> Adriana is a doctor? But **she's so young**!
>
> **SYNONYM:** **oler a polvo de talco** *exp.* • (lit.): to smell like baby powder.

patán *m.* rude man.

> example:
> Antonio es un **patán**. Yo no entiendo cómo lo aguanta su esposa.
>
> translation:
> Antonio is a **jerk**. I don't understand how his wife can stand him.
>
> **SYNONYM:** **sangrón** *m.* an obnoxious man • (lit.): bloody.

película equis *exp.* dirty movie, X-rated movie • (lit.): X movie.

> example:
> ¡Esos niños son demasiado jóvenes para ver **películas equis**!
>
> translation:
> These children are too young to see **dirty movies**!
>
> **SYNONYM:** **película colorada** *exp.* • (lit.): red movie.

presa fácil *f.* easy lay • (lit.): easy prey.

> example:
> Andrea tiene fama de ser **presa fácil**. Siempre tiene al menos tres novios.
>
> translation:
> Andrea has a reputation of being an **easy lay**. She always has at least three boyfriends.
>
> **VARIATION:** **fácil** *adj.* easy • *Esa chica es muy fácil;* That girl is very easy.

tener una boda por todo lo alto *exp.* to have a big (elegant) wedding • (lit.): to have a very high wedding.

> example:
> Augusto y Ana **tuvieron una boda por todo lo alto**. ¡Les debe de haber costado una fortuna!
>
> translation:
> Augusto and Ana **had a huge wedding**. It must have cost them a fortune!
>
> **NOTE:** This expression can also be used with any other kind of party or celebration.

viejo rabo verde *exp.* dirty old man • (lit.): old green tail.

> example:
> Rodolfo es un **viejo rabo verde**. Tiene ochenta años y todavía le gustan las mujeres jóvenes.
>
> translation:
> Rodolfo is a **dirty old man**. He's eighty years old and he stills loves young women.

A CLOSER LOOK:
Dating Terms at Your Fingertips

Since Latins are certainly known for being the consummate romantics, it seems only logical to begin by presenting some of the most common terms used in courting. Once you have been armed with the following arsenal of expressions and slang terms, you will surely be ready to *echar los perros* ("to flirt," literally "to throw dogs").

Boyfriend

novio *m.* • (lit.): bridegroom, fiancé.

example:
¿Conoces a mi **novio**? Creo que nos vamos a casar algún día.

translation:
Did you meet my **boyfriend**? I think we're going to get married someday.

Caress

acariciar *v.* • (lit.): to caress, touch lightly.

example:
Durante la película, ¡José empezó a **acariciarme** el cuello!

translation:
During the movie, José started **to caress me** on my neck!

caricia *f.* • (lit.): caress.

example:
Mi mamá me dio una **caricia** en la cabeza cuando yo estaba enojado. Eso me tranquilizó en seguida.

translation:
My mother gave me a **caress** on my head when I was so upset. That calmed me down right away.

Dirty magazine

revista equis *f.* • (lit.): an X(-rated) magazine.

example:
¡Encontré una **revista equis** en el cuarto de mi hermano pequeño! Me pregunto dónde la consiguió.

translation:
I found a **dirty magazine** in my little brother's bedroom! I wonder where he found it.

Dirty movie

película equis *f.* • (lit.): an X(-rated) movie.

example:
¡No podemos llevar a los niños a ver eso...es una **película equis**!

translation:
We can't take the children to see that...it's an **X-rated movie**!

Dirty old man

viejo rabo verde *m.* • (lit.): old green tail.

example:
¡Ese hombre está saliendo con una mujer veinte años más joven que él! Yo creo que es un **viejo rabo verde**.

translation:
That man is dating a girl twenty years younger than he is! I think he's just a **dirty old man**.

Dump someone (to)

dar calabazas a alguien *exp.*
• (lit.): to give pumpkins to someone.

example:
Yo pensé que Carlos y yo nos íbamos a casar, y de repente sin ninguna razón, ¡**me dio calabazas**!

translation:
I thought Carlos and I were going to get married. Then for no reason, **he dumped me**!

dejar a alguien *exp.* • (lit.): to leave someone.

example:
Sandra **me dejó** por otro tipo.

translation:
Sandra **dumped me** for another guy.

dejar a alguien a su suerte *exp.* • (lit.): to leave someone to his/her luck.

example:
El día de nuestra boda, ¡Manuel **me dejó a mi suerte**!

translation:
On our wedding day, Manuel **dumped me**!

plantar a alguien *exp.*
• (lit.): to throw someone out.

example:
¿Has oido la noticia? Verónica **dejó plantado** a Pedro porque ¡lo agarró con otra mujer!

translation:
Did you hear the news? Veronica **dumped Pedro** because she caught him with another woman!

Easy lay (to be an)

bollo loco *m. (Cuba)*
• (lit.): crazy bread roll or bun.

example:
Ana se acuesta con un tipo diferente cada noche. Es un **bollo loco**.

translation:
Ana has sex with a different guy every night. She's a **real easy lay**.

NOTE: In Cuba, *bollo* ("bread roll" or "bun") is used to refer to "vagina."

chapete *f.*

example:
Me pregunto si Elvia querrá salir conmigo. He oído que es una **chapete**.

translation:
I wonder if Elvia will go out with me. I hear she's a **real easy lay**.

cogetuda *f.* *(Argentina).*

example:
Laura es famosa por ser **cogetuda**. Los hombres siempre quieren salir con ella.

translation:
Laura is known for being **an easy lay**. Guys always want to go out with her.

NOTE: This is from the verb *coger* meaning (in many Spanish-speaking countries) "to fuck."

de vida fácil *exp.* • (lit.): of an easy (or loose) life.

example:
Emilio tiene muchas novias. Verdaderamente, es un hombre **de vida fácil**.

translation:
Emilio has a lot of girlfriends. He certainly does have **an active sex life**.

fácil *adj.* • (lit.): easy.

example:
Vilma parecerá inocente, pero en realidad es **fácil**.

translation:
Vilma may look innocent, but she's really **easy**.

facilito/a *n. & adj.* easy lay; easy • (lit.): a little easy one.

example:
Clarissa es una **facilita**. Se acuesta con un tipo diferente cada noche.

translation:
Clarissa is an **easy lay**. She has sex with a different guy every night.

piruja *n. & adj.* easy lay; easy • (lit.): vulgar for "slut."

example:
Elvia es una **piruja**. Ella duerme con todo el mundo.

translation:
Elvia is a **slut**. She has sex with everyone.

presa fácil (ser una) *f.*
• (lit.): to be an easy grab.

example:
Estoy seguro de que Inés se acostará contigo; es famosa por ser **presa fácil**.

translation:
I'm sure Inés will have sex with you. She's known as **an easy lay**.

Engaged (to be)

comprometido/a (estar) *adj.*
• (lit.): to be compromised.

example:
Acabo de enterarme de que estás **comprometido**. ¡Enhorabuena!

translation:
I just found out that you're **engaged**. Congratulations!

Flirt (to)

echar los perros *exp.*
• (lit.): to throw dogs.

example:
Siempre que Alfonso ve a una mujer guapa, empieza a **echarle los perros**.

translation:
Every time Alfonso sees a pretty girl, he starts **to flirt**.

Girlfriend

novia *f.* • (lit.): bride, fiancée.

example:
¿Esa es tu **novia**? ¡Enhorabuena! ¡Es muy simpática y tan bonita!

translation:
That's your **girlfriend**? Congratulations! She's very nice and so beautiful!

Go out on a date (to)

salir con alguien *exp.*
• (lit.): to go out with someone.

example:
Voy a **salir con** Silvia mañana por la noche. ¿Puedes recomendarme un buen restaurante?

translation:
I'm **going out with** Silvia tomorrow night. Can you suggest a good restaurant?

Have more than one girlfriend (to)

andar con otra *exp.*
• (lit.): to walk with another female.

example:
Sé que te gusta Paulo, pero ten cuidado. **Anda con otra**.

translation:
I know you like Paulo, but be careful. **He has more than one girlfriend**.

*Have more than
one boyfriend (to)*

andar con otro *exp.* • (lit.): to walk with another male.

example:
Iba a pedirle a Berta que se casara conmigo, pero me acabo de enterar de que ¡**anda con otro**!

translation:
I was going to ask Berta to marry me, but I just found out she's **going with someone else**!

Hot chick

buenona *f. (Spain).*

example:
¿Has visto a esa **buenona** que sale con Juan? ¡Es preciosa!

translation:
Did you see the **hot chick** Juan is going out with? She's beautiful!

NOTE: This is from the feminine adjective *buena* meaning "good."

chava bien [buena] *f.* •
(lit.): young girl well good.

example:
Mira a esa **chava bien [buena]**. Me pregunto si ella es un modelo.

translation:
Look at that **hot girl**. I wonder if she's a model.

maja *f.* • (lit.): elegant woman, belle.

example:
¿Has visto a Sandra? ¡Ella es muy **maja**!

translation:
Have you see Sandra? She's a really **elegant woman**!

SEE: *majo, p. 16.*

mango *m.* • (lit.): mango.

example:
¡Mi maestra de biología es un **mango**!

translation:
My biology teacher is a **hot number**!

merengue *f. (Spain)*
• (lit.): meringue (since *meringue* is so sweet).

example:
¿Ves a ese **merengue** allí? ¡Creo que te está mirando!

translation:
See that **hot chick** over there? I think she's looking at you!

pinchón *m.* • (lit.): small bird.

example:
Todos los chavos en la escuela piensan que mi hermana es todo un **pichón**.

translation:
All the guys in school think my sister is a real **hot chick**.

NOTE: The masculine noun *chavo* (used in the example above) is a very popular term in Mexico meaning "guy."

tía buena *f. (Spain)* • (lit.): good aunt.

example:
Tu hermana pequeña se ha convertido en una verdadera **tía buena**.

translation:
Your little sister has really turned into a **hot chick**.

NOTE: The feminine noun *tía* is commonly used in Spain to mean "woman" or "girl."

Huge wedding
(to have a)

tener una boda por todo lo alto *exp.* • (lit.): to have a wedding for all the high.

example:
Cuando me case, voy a **tener una boda por todo lo alto**.

translation:
When I get married, I'm going **to have a huge wedding**.

Hunk

chavo bien [bueno] *m.* • (lit.): young guy well good.

example:
¡Tu hermano es un **chavo bien [bueno]**!

translation:
Your brother is a **hunk**!

chulo *m. (Spain)* • (lit.): • **1.** bull-fighter's assistant • **2.** pimp.

example:
¿Has visto al nuevo estudiante? ¡Es un verdadero **chulo**!

translation:
Did you see the new student? He's such a **hunk**!

cuero *m. & adj.* hunk; hunky • (lit.): leather.

example:
Tu hermano es tan **cuero**. ¿Tiene novia?

translation:
Your brother is so **hunky**.
Does he have a girlfriend?

majo *m.* • (lit.): elegant man,
beau.

example:
¿Crees que David es un **majo**?

translation:
Do you believe that David is a
classy guy?

mango *m.* • (lit.): mango.

example:
Tu hermano es muy sexy. ¡Qué
mango!

translation:
Your brother is very sexy.
What a **hunk**!

papasito *m. & adj.* a hot daddy;
sexy • (lit.): little father.

example:
Carlos tiene muchas novias. Es
un **papasito**!

translation:
Carlos has a lot of girfriends.
He's such a **hunk**!

In love (to be)

enamoradísimo/a (estar)
adj. • (lit.): to be super
enamored.

example:
Creo que David está
enamoradísimo de su
profesora de piano.

translation:
I think David is **big-time
in love** with his piano
teacher.

Lead someone on (to)

insinuarse a alguien *exp.*
• (lit.): to hint oneself to
someone.

example:
Tienes que dejar de
insinuarte a él y ser
honesta con tus
sentimientos.

translation:
You need to **stop leading
him on** and be honest
about your feelings.

ojitos (hacer) *exp.* • (lit.): to
make little eyes.

example:
Creo que Ricardo te está
haciendo ojitos porque
ayer le ví en el cine con otra
chica.

translation:
I think Ricardo is **leading
you on** because yesterday
I saw him at the movies with
another girl.

Love at first sight

amor a primera vista *exp.*
• (lit.): love at first sight.

example:
Cuando se conocieron mis padres, fue **amor a primera vista**.

translation:
When my parents met each other, it was **love at first sight**.

Make out (to)

darse el lote *exp. (Spain)*
• (lit.): to give each other the portion or allotment (of kisses).

example:
¿Sabías que Marco y Alicia salían? Les he visto hoy **dándose el lote** en el parque.

translation:
Did you know that Marco and Alicia were going out? I saw them **making out** in the park today.

darse una buena calentada
exp. (Mexico) • (lit.): to give each other a good heating up.

example:
¡Ven rápido! ¡Carol y Humberto se están **dando una buena calentada** en público!

translation:
Come quickly! Carol and Humberto are **making out** in public!

Play footsie (to)

manitas (hacer) *exp.*

example:
No pienso volver a salir con Eric. ¡Empezó a **hacer manitas** conmigo en el restaurante!

translation:
I'm never going out with Eric again. He started **playing footsie** with me at the restaurant!

NOTE: This is from the feminine noun *mano* meaning "hand" or "paw."

Playboy (to be a)

Don Juan (ser un) *m.*
• (lit.): to be a Don Juan (a fictitious character known for being a womanizer).

example:
¿Estás saliendo con Ricardo? Ese hombre es un **Don Juan**. ¡Tiene un montón de novias!

translation:
You're going out with Ricardo? That guy's such a **playboy**. He has tons of girlfriends!

mujeriego *m. & adj.*
  skirt-chaser; obsessed with
  women • (lit.): one who is
  obsessed with women (from
  the feminine noun *mujer*
  meaning "woman").

  example:
  Nunca saldría con alguien tan
  mujeriego como Simón. No
  creo que él pudiera ser fiel.

  translation:
  I would never go out with such
  a **skirt-chaser** as Simón.
  I don't think he could ever
  be faithful.

Rob the cradle (to)

gustar los bebes *exp.*
  • (lit.): to like babies.

  example:
  Roberto siempre sale con
  mujeres mucho más jóvenes
  que él. Yo creo que le **gustan
  los bebes**.

  translation:
  Roberto always dates women
  much younger than he is.
  I think he likes **to rob the
  cradle**.

Sex on the brain (to have)

enfermo sexual (ser un) *m.*
  • (lit.): to be a sexually corrupt
  person.

  example:
  Juan siempre está pensando
  en el sexo. Yo creo que es
  un **enfermo sexual**.

  translation:
  All Juan ever thinks about is
  sex. I think he's a **sex
  maniac**.

Stand someone up (to)

dejar clavado/a *exp.*
  • (lit.): to leave nailed (in
  one place).

  example:
  Llevo una hora esperando
  aquí. ¡No me puedo creer
  que Guillermo me haya
  dejado clavada!

  translation:
  I've been waiting here for
  an hour. I can't believe that
  Guillermo **stood me up**!

dejar plantado/a *exp.*
  • (lit.): to leave planted.

  example:
  ¿Llevas dos horas esperando
  a Marco? Creo que deberías
  marcharte. Me temo que **te
  ha dejado plantada**.

  translation:
  You've been waiting for
  Marco for two hours? I think
  you should just leave. I'm
  afraid he's **stood you up**.

Tie the knot (to)

arrimarse *v.* • (lit.): to shelve oneself (and be in circulation no longer).

example:
¡Enhorabuena! He oído que ¡**se van a arrimar** la semana que viene!

translation:
Congratulations! I heard that **you're going to tie the knot** next week!

atar el nudo *exp.* • (lit.): to tie the knot.

example:
Después de diez años, ¡Rodolfo y Julia van a **atar el nudo**!

translation:
After ten years, Rodolfo and Julia are finally going **to tie the knot**!

cometer la equivocación *exp.* • (lit.): to make the mistake.

example:
Antonio finalmente ha decidido **cometer la equivocación**.

translation:
Antonio has finally decided **to get married**.

tomar mujer *exp.* • (lit.): to take a woman.

example:
¿David ha **tomado mujer**? Creí que le gustaba ser un solterón.

translation:
David **got married**? I thought he enjoyed being a bachelor.

ALSO: tomar hombre *exp.* to get married to a man • (lit.): to take a man.

¡Roberto *me vuelve loco*! ¡Yo creo que está *loco de remate*!

(trans.): Robert **drives me crazy**! I think he's **out of his mind**!
(lit.): Robert **drives me crazy**! I think he's **crazy to the end**!

Ana: ¡Mira! Ese es el **enano** de Roberto. Tengo el presentimiento de que te sigue a todas partes.

Marco: ¡Oye! ¡**Cierra el pico**! ¿Sabes que nadie lo aguanta en el trabajo porque es un verdadero **pelota**? Si tú llegas tarde alguna vez, él se lo dice al **latoso** del jefe. No solo eso, sino que a él **no le importa un carajo** su trabajo. El pasa la mayor parte del día **contando chismes** a sus amigos por teléfono. Te digo, es un verdadero **huevón**.

Ana: Yo nunca saldría con un **gordinflón** como ese. ¡Es un **pélon horroroso** y **le apesta la boca!** Además es un **tostón** y un **farolero**.

Marco: ¡Es un **cretino**! ¡Me **vuelve loco**! ¡Yo creo que está **loco de remate**!

Robert drives me crazy! I think he's out of his mind!

Ana: Hey! There's that **runt** Roberto. I get the feeling that he follows you around everywhere.

Marco: Geez! **Shut your trap**! Did you know that no one can stand him at work either because he's such a **brown-noser**? If you ever arrive late, he reports you to our **pain-in-the-neck** boss. Not only that, but he **doesn't give a damn** about his own work. He spends most of the day **gossiping** on the telephone with his friends. I'm telling you, he's a real **lazy bum**.

Ana: I'd never go out with a **tub of lard** like that. He's a **horrible-looking bald guy** and has **bad breath**! He's also a **jerk** and a **braggart**.

Marco: He's a **cretin**! He **drives me crazy**! I think he's **out of his mind**!

Vocabulary

apestar la boca *exp.* to have bad breath • (lit.): to have a stinky mouth.

example:
A Mario le **apesta la boca** porque siempre está fumando.

translation:
Mario **has bad breath** because he's always smoking.

cerrar el pico *exp.* to shut up, "to shut one's trap" • (lit.): to close/shut the beak.

example:
¡No te quiero oír más! ¡**Cierra el pico**!

translation:
I don't want to hear any more out of you! **Shut up**!

SYNONYM -1: ¡**Cállate!** *v.* Shut up!

SYNONYM -2: **cerrar la boca** *exp.* : to close/shut the mouth.

contar chismes *exp.* to gossip • (lit.): to tell stories.

example:
Nunca le digas a Eduardo nada personal. A él le encanta **contar chismes**.

translation:
Don't ever tell Eduardo anything personal. He loves **to gossip**.

SYNONYM: **chismear** *v.* • (lit.): to gossip.

cretino/a *n. & adj.* jerk, cretin; jerky • (lit.): cretin.

example:
Juan es un **cretino**. No sabe ni cómo atarse sus propios zapatos.

translation:
Juan is a **cretin**. He doesn't even know how to tie his own shoes.

enano/a *n. & adj.* short person, runt; "runty" • (lit.): dwarf, midget.

example:
¿Javier quiere ser jugador de baloncesto? ¡Pero si es un verdadero **enano**!

translation:
Javier wants to be a basketball player? But he's such a **runt**!

VARIATION: **enanito/a** *n.* • (lit.): little dwarf.

farolero/a *n.* braggart, showoff • (lit.): lantern maker or vendor.

example:
¿Viste todas las joyas que traía puesta Esperanza en la fiesta? ¡Es toda una **farolera**!

translation:
Did you see all the expensive jewelry Esperanza was wearing at the party? She's such a **showoff**!

gordinflón/ona *n. & adj.* tub of lard, fat slob, fatso; fat • (lit.): from the adjective *gordo/a* meaning "fat."

example:
David es un verdadero **gordinflón**. Parece que siempre está comiendo.

translation:
David is such a **fat slob**. It seems like he's always eating.

SYNONYM -1: **ballena** *f.* • (lit.): whale.

SYNONYM -2: **vaca** *f.* • (lit.): cow.

horroroso/a *adj.* horrible, very ugly person • (lit.): horrible, dreadful, frightful.

example:
El novio de Margarita es **horroroso**. La verdad es que no sé qué verá en él.

translation:
Margarita's boyfriend is **really ugly**. The truth is I don't know what
she sees in him.

huevón *n. & adj.* lazy bum; lazy • (lit.): big egg.

example:
Mi jefe es un **huevón**. Siempre tengo que hacer su trabajo.

translation:
My boss is such a **lazy retch**. I always have to do his work.

latoso/a *n. & adj.* pain-in-the-neck; annoying • (lit.): made of tin can.

example:
Ese bebé es un **latoso**. Nunca deja de llorar.

translation:
That baby is a real **pain-in-the-neck**. He never stops crying.

loco/a de remate *exp.* out of one's mind • (lit.): crazy all the way to
the end.

example:
Ese tipo está **loco de remate**. ¡Lleva los zapatos en las orejas!

translation:
That guy is **out of his mind**. He's wearing his shoes on his ears!

SYNONYM -1: **faltar un tornillo** *exp.* • (lit.): to be missing a
screw.

SYNONYM -2: **loco/a como una cabra** *exp.* • (lit.): crazy like a
goat.

no importar un carajo *exp.* not to give a damn • (lit.): not to
mind a penis.

example:
No me importa un carajo si quieres ir a la fiesta conmigo o no.

translation:
I don't give a damn whether you want to go to the party with me
or not.

> **SYNONYM -1:**   **no importar un bledo** *exp.* • (lit.): not to mind a blade or leaf.

> **SYNONYM -2:**   **no importar un comino** *exp.* • (lit.): not to mind a cumin clove.

pelón/ona *n. & adj.* baldy; bald • (lit.): hairless.

example:
Me temo que voy a ser **pelón**, porque mi padre perdió todo el pelo en su veintena.

translation:
I'm afraid I'm going to be **bald** because my father lost all of his hair when he was in his twenties.

pelota *f.* brown-noser • (lit.): ball.

example:
Alejandro es una verdadera **pelota**. Siempre está de acuerdo con lo que dice el maestro.

translation:
Alejandro is such a **brown-noser**. He always agrees with everything the teacher says.

> **NOTE:**   In Colombia, the term *pelota* means "stupid."

> **SYNONYM -1:**   **barbero** *m.* • (lit.): barber.

> **SYNONYM -2:**   **lamesuelas** *n.* • (lit.): one who licks shoe soles.

tostón/ona *n. & adj.* pain-in-the-neck, boring thing or person; annoying • (lit.): large piece of toast.

example:
El discurso de Jorge fue un verdadero **tostón**. Creí que me iba a quedar dormido.

translation:
Jorge's speech was a real **bore**. I thought I was going to fall asleep.

volver loco a alguien *exp.* to drive someone crazy • (lit.): to turn someone crazy.

example:
Andrés **me vuelve loco** porque nunca deja de hablar.

translation:
Andrés **drives me crazy** because he never stops talking.

A CLOSER LOOK:
Nonvulgar Insults & Putdowns

Learning popular insults can prove to be extremely handy for those little annoying moments when you need to spout off a good retort as well as being able to recognize when you have been insulted by someone. This following list is sure to get you ready for just about any situation.

Bad breath (to have)

apestar la boca *exp.* • (lit.): to stink from the mouth.

example:
Yo creo que Ernie nunca se lava los dientes. ¡Siempre le **apesta la boca**!

translation:
I don't think Ernie ever brushes his teeth. He always has **horrible breath**!

Bald

calco *m.* • (lit.): tracing (drawing).

example:
¿Conoces a Ernesto? ¡Es **calco** y sólo tiene diecisiete años!

translation:
Do you know Ernesto? He's **bald** and he's only seventeen years old!

calvito *adj.*

example:
Me temo que voy a ser **calvito**, porque mi padre perdió todo el pelo en su veintena.

translation:
I'm afraid I'm going to be **bald** because my father lost all of his hair when he was in his twenties.

NOTE: This is from the adjective *calvo* meaning "bald."

pelón/ona *n. & adj.* baldy; bald.

example:
Enrique tiene solamente diez y seis años y él ya está **pelón**.

translation:
Enrique is only sixteen years old and he's already **bald**.

Blabbermouth / Gossip

bocón/ona *n. & adj.*
blabbermouth; gossipy • (lit.): big-mouthed.

example:
Estuve hablando por teléfono con Susana más de una hora. ¡Es una **bocona**!

translation:
I was on the telephone with Susana for an hour. She's such a **blabbermouth**!

NOTE: This is from the feminine noun *boca* meaning "mouth."

chismolero/a *n. & adj.* one who spreads gossip or *chismes*; gossipy.

example:
No te creas nada de lo que dice Ana. ¡Qué **chismolera**!

translation:
Don't believe anything Ana says. What a **gossip**!

chismoso/a *n.* one who spreads gossip or *chismes*.

example:
No le cuentes a Jorge nada personal. Es un **chismoso**.

translation:
Don't tell anything personal to Jorge. He's a **gossip**.

comadrera *f.* blabbermouth.

example:
¿Cómo sabías que me iba a casar?¿Te lo dijo la **comadrera** de Cristina?

translation:
How did you know I was getting married? Did that **blabbermouth** Christina tell you?

NOTE: This is from the feminine noun *comadre* meaning "gossip."

cotorra *f.* • (lit.): parrot.

example:
¡Le conté un secreto a Ana y se lo contó a todo el mundo! Se me había olvidado lo **cotorra** que es.

translation:
I told a secret to Ana and she told everyone! I forgot what a **blabbermouth** she is.

cuentero/a *n. & adj.*
(*Argentina*) a gossip; gossipy• (lit.): one who tells tales.

example:
¿Le contaste un secreto a Antonio? No fue buena idea. Es todo un **cuentero**.

translation:
You told Antonio a secret? That wasn't a good idea. He's such a **blabbermouth**.

enredador/a *n. (Spain)* a gossip • (lit.): meddler.

example:
Le conté a Armando todos mis problemas personales y se lo contó a todos sus amigos. ¡Nunca volveré a confiar en ese **enredador**!

translation:
I told Armando all about my personal problems and he told all of his friends. I'll never trust that **blabbermouth** again!

enredoso/a *n. & adj. (Chile, Mexico)* a gossip; gossipy • (lit.): fraught with difficulties.

example:
A Mateo le encanta expandir rumores. Es un **enredoso**.

translation:
Mateo likes to spread rumors. He's a **gossip**.

farandulero/a *n. & adj.* a gossip; gossipy • (lit.): actor, strolling player.

example:
Benito y yo éramos buenos amigos hasta que descubrí que era un **farandulero**. No puedo volver a confiar en él.

translation:
Benito and I used to be good friends until I discovered that he was a **gossip**. I can never trust him again.

gritón/ona *n. & adj.*
loudmouth; gossipy.

example:
Habla bajo. Esto es una biblioteca. ¡Eres un **gritón**!

translation:
Keep your voice down. This is a library. You're such a **loudmouth**!

NOTE: This is from the verb *gritar* meaning "to shout."

hocicón/ona *n. & adj.*
loudmouth; gossipy • (lit.): mouthy (since this term comes from the masculine noun *hocico* meaning "snout").

example:
No quiero invitar a Anita a mi fiesta porque no la soporto. ¡Es tan **hocicona**!

translation:
I don't want to invite Anita to my party because I can't stand her. She's such a **loudmouth**!

lengua larga (tener) *exp.*
(Argentina) • (lit.): to have a long tongue.

example:
A Angel le encanta chismear de la gente. **Tiene la lengua larga**.

translation:
Angel loves to gossip about people. **He's a blabber-mouth**.

lenguasuelta *n. & adj. (Mexico)*
a gossip; gossipy • (lit.): loose tongue.

example:
¡Para de ser **lenguasuelta**! No son mas que mentiras.

translation:
Stop being a **gossip**! Those are nothing but lies.

lenguatuda *f. (Argentina)*
• (lit.): one with a long tongue (used for blabbing).

example:
Consuela no puede guardar un secreto. Es una **lenguatuda**.

translation:
Consuela can't keep a secret. She's such a **blabbermouth**.

hablador/a *n. & adj.*
blabbermouth; gossipy.

example:
¿Le contaste a Jesús mi secreto? ¡Qué **hablador**!

translation:
You told Jesús my secret? What a **blabbermouth**!

NOTE: This is from the verb *hablar* meaning "to speak."

mitotero/a *n. & adj.* a gossip; gossipy • (lit.): rowdy, noisy person.

example:
Te lo advierto, Margarita es una verdadera **mitotera**. No le cuentes nada personal.

translation:
I'm warning you. Margarita is a real **gossip**. Don't tell her anything personal.

parlanchín m. blabbermouth
• (lit.): talkative.

example:
Armando habla sin parar. Es un **parlanchín**.

translation:
Armando talks nonstop. He's a **blabbermouth**.

trompudo/a n. & adj. big-mouthed person.

example:
Alejandro no para de hablar. Es un **trompudo**.

translation:
Alejandro never stops talking. He's such a **big-mouth**.

NOTE: This is from the feminine noun *trompa* meaning "elephant's trunk" or the musical instrument the "horn."

Boring (to be)

pesado/a n. & adj. a bore; boring • (lit.): heavy.

example:
El discurso de David fue **pesado**.

translation:
David's lecture was **boring**.

petardo (ser un) m.
• (lit.): to be a torpedo, firecracker.

example:
No me gusta estar con Miguel. ¡Es tan **petardo**!

translation:
I don't like spending time with Miguel. He's such a **bore**!

tostón m. • (lit.): anything overtoasted (and therefore unwanted).

example:
Nuestro nuevo profesor de biología es un **tostón**. Me es difícil mantenerme despierto en su clase.

translation:
Our new biology teacher is such a **bore**. I have trouble staying awake in his class.

Brown-nose (to) / Brown-noser

hacer la barba exp.
• (lit.): to do the beard.

example:
La razón por la que Ricardo ha conseguido un ascenso es porque siempre está **haciendo la barba**.

translation:
The reason Ricardo got a promotion is because he's such a **brown-noser**.

hacer la pelotilla *exp.*
- (lit.): to do the testicle or "lick someone's balls" (since *pelotilla*, literally meaning "small balls," is used in Spanish slang to mean "small testicles").

example:
David ha debido **hacer la pelotilla** para conseguir que le subieran el sueldo.

translation:
David must have **brown-nosed** to get a raise.

lameculo[s] *m. & adj.*
- (lit.): butt-licker.

example:
¿Has oido cómo le hablaba Ana al jefe? Nunca supe que fuera tan **lameculo[s]**.

translation:
Did you hear how Ana was talking to the boss? I never knew she was such a **kiss-ass**.

lamesuelas *m. & adj.*
- (lit.): leather licker.

example:
La razón por la que al jefe le gusta tanto Victor es porque éste es un **lamesuelas**.

translation:
The reason the boss likes Victor so much is because he's such a **kiss-ass**.

pelota *n. & adj.* • (lit.): ball (or one who "licks someone's balls or testicles").

example:
El único motivo por el que Roberto fue ascendido, es porque es un **pelota**.

translation:
The only reason Roberto got a promotion is because he's a **kiss-ass**.

ALSO: pelota *adj.*
(Colombia) stupid.

Crazy (to be)

enfermo mental (ser un) *exp.* • (lit.): to be a mentally corrupt person.

example:
No me puedo creer que Cynthia vaya a ser madre. ¡Es una **enferma mental**!

translation:
I can't believe Cynthia is going to be a mother. She's such a **mental case**!

faltar un tornillo *exp.*
• (lit.): to be missing a screw.

example:
Mi psiquiatra habla solo todo el rato. Yo creo que **le falta un tornillo**.

translation:
My psychiatrist talks to himself all the time. I think **he has a screw loose**.

loco/a como una cabra (estar) *exp.* • (lit.): to be as crazy as a nanny goat.

example:
Si yo fuera tú no confiaría en él. ¡Está **loco como una cabra**!

translation:
I wouldn't trust him if I were you. He's **out of his mind**!

loco/a de remate (estar) *exp.*
• (lit.): to be crazy to the end.

example:
Si piensas que voy a salir con Manuel, ¡es que estás **loco de remate**!

translation:
If you think I'm going to go out with Manuel, you're **nuts**!

Drive someone crazy (to)

sacar de quicio a alguien
exp. • (lit.): to bring someone to his/her threshold (of tolerance).

example:
¡Los nuevos vecinos hacen tanto ruido! ¡**Me sacan de quicio**!

translation:
The new neighbors are making so much noise! **They're driving me crazy**!

volver loco/a a alguien
exp. to drive someone crazy
• (lit.): to turn someone crazy.

example:
El tráfico de esta ciudad me está **volviendo loco**.

translation:
All the traffic in this city is **making me crazy**.

Drunk(ard)

bolo *m. (Nicaragua, El Salvador)* • (lit.): skittle.

example:
Eduardo tiene un problema con la bebida. Creo que es un **bolo**.

translation:
Eduardo has a problem with alcohol. I think he's a **drunk**.

borrachal m. (from the adjective *borracho/a* meaning "drunk").

example:
David no puede encontrar trabajo porque todo el mundo sabe que es un **borrachal**.

translation:
David can't get a job because everyone knows he's a **drunk**.

borrachón/ona f. & adj. (*Argentina*) • (lit.): big drunkard.

example:
Como siempre, Marco bebió demasiado en mi fiesta. ¡Es un **borrachón**!

translation:
As usual, Marco had too much to drink at my party. He's such a **drunk**!

bufa f. (*Cuba*) • (lit.): jest, piece of buffoonery.

example:
Yo no sabía que Antonio era un **bufa**. Ayer se presentó al trabajo con una botella de vino en la mano.

translation:
I didn't know Antonio was such a **drunk**. Yesterday he showed up at work holding a wine bottle.

chupandín m. (*Argentina*) • (lit.): big sucker (from the verb *chupar* meaning "to suck").

example:
¿Viste cuánto alcohol bebió Jack ayer por la noche? ¡No tenía ni idea de que fuera tan **chupandín**!

translation:
Did you see how much alcohol Jack drank last night? I had no idea he was such a **lush**!

codo empinado m. • (lit.): tilted elbow.

example:
¡Nunca me había dado cuenta de que Francisco era un **codo empinado**! ¿Has visto cuánto vino tomó durante la cena?

translation:
I never realized what a **drunk** Francisco was! Did you see how much wine he drank during dinner?

cuete (ponerse) adj. to get drunk • (lit.): slice of rump (of beef).

example:
Benito nunca parece
demasiado sano. Yo creo
que **se pone cuete** todo
el tiempo.

translation:
Benito never looks very
healthy. I think he **gets
drunk** all the time.

engazado/a *adj.* • (lit.): gassed
up.

example:
Ricardo se puso **engazado** a
mi fiesta.

translation:
Ricardo got **plastered** at my
party.

manudo/a *n. (El Salvador)*
drunkard.

example:
No pienso volver a invitar al
manudo de Rafael a mi casa
nunca más. ¡Fue tan
vergonzoso!

translation:
I'm never inviting that
drunkard Rafael to my
house again. He was so
embarrassing!

pipa *f.* • (lit.): pipe (for smoking
tobacco).

example:
¡Qué lástima! Acabo de
descubrir que la madre de
Emilio es una **pipa**.

translation:
What a shame! I just found
out that Emilio's mother is a
drunkard.

pisto/a *adj.* drunk, bombed
• (lit.): chicken broth.

example:
Si me tomo media copa de
vino, estoy **pista**.

translation:
If I drink half a glass of wine,
I get **bombed**.

tecolote *m.* • (lit.): owl.

example:
Mira a ese **tecolote** de allí.
¡Creo que es mi profesor de
biología!

translation:
Look at that **drunkard**
over there. I think that's my
biology teacher!

tronado/a *adj. (El Salvador)*
• (lit.): spoiled.

example:
¿Cómo te has podido beber
todo el vaso de Vodka? ¡Yo
estaría totalmente
tronado!

translation:
How did you drink that entire glass of Vodka? I'd be totally **bombed**!

Fat slob

botija n. & adj. fat slob; chunky, fat • (lit.): short-necked earthen jug.

example:
A mí me daría verguenza salir con esa **botija**.

translation:
I would be embarrassed to go out with that **fat slob**.

chancho m. • (lit.): fat pig.

example:
Ese **chancho** se acaba de comer siete hamburguesas. No me sorprende que está así.

translation:
That **fat slob** just ate seven hamburgers. It doesn't surprise me he looks like that.

¡Ché gordo, te vas a reventar! exp. (Argentina) in response to seeing someone very fat • (lit.): Hey fatso, you're going to explode!

example:
¡Ché gordo, te vas a reventar! ¡Deja de comerte esa tarta!

translation:
Hey fatso, you're going to explode! Stop eating that cake!

comelón/ona n. & adj. one who eats a lot, pig; piggy.

example:
¿Has visto todo lo que se ha comido Alfonso para almorzar? ¡Qué **comelón**!

translation:
Did you see how much food Alfonso ate during lunch? What a **pig**!

NOTE: This is from the verb *comer* meaning "to eat."

cuchi m. • (lit.): variation of *cochino* meaning "filthy."

example:
Como te comas todo eso, te vas a poner **cuchi**.

translation:
If you eat all that, you're going to become a **fat pig**.

elefante m. & adj. fatso; fat • (lit.): elephant.

example:
Después de comer tanto dulce, me siento como un **elefante**.

translation:
After eating so much dessert, I feel like a **fat pig**.

NOTE: Although this is a masculine noun, it can be applied to a woman as well.

foca f. (Spain) • (lit.): seal.

example:
No pienso ponerme ese bañador. ¡Parezco una **foca**!

translation:
I'm not going to wear that bathing suit. It makes me look like a **fat cow**!

gordinflón/ona n. & adj. fatso; fat.

example:
Solía ser un **gordinflón**, pero después de mucha dieta y ejercicio, finalmente estoy en forma.

translation:
I used to be a **fat pig**, but after a lot of dieting and exercise, I'm finally in perfect shape.

NOTE: This is from the adjective gordo meaning "fat."

gordo/a chancho n. & adj. (Argentina) fatso; fat
• (lit.): fat hog-like person.

example:
Nuestro jefe es un **gordo chancho**. No sé por qué no se pone a dieta.

translation:
Our new boss is a **fat pig**. I don't know why he doesn't go on a diet.

gordo/a de mierda n. (Argentina) fatso • (lit.): fat one of shit.

example:
¡Qué **gordo de mierda**! Ese tipo nunca para de comer.

translation:
What a **fat pig**! That guy never stops eating.

jamón/ona n. & adj. fatso; fat
• (lit.): ham.

example:
¡Vaya **jamona**! ¡Debe pesar una tonelada!

translation:
What a **fatso**! She must weigh a ton!

panzón/ona n. & adj. fat slob; chubby, fat.

example:
Cecila estaba tan delgada. Ahora es una **panzona**.

translation:
Cecilia used to be so thin. Now she's a **fat slob**.

panzudo al pedo adj.
(Argentina) • (lit.): paunchy to the fart.

example:
Mi tío es **panzudo al pedo**. ¡Le encanta comer!

translation:
My uncle is **fat out to here**. He loves to eat!

puerco/a n. & adj. (Argentina)
• (lit.): pig.

example:
¿Te has comido la tarta entera? ¡Qué **puerco**!

translation:
You ate that entire cake? What a **pig**!

troncho/a n. & adj.
(El Salvador) fatso; fat
• (lit.): stalk, stem.

example:
Me voy a poner **troncho** como no me ponga a dieta.

translation:
I'm going to get **fat** if I don't go on a diet.

tunco/a n. & adj. (El Salvador)
fatso; fat • (lit.): (Honduras, Mexico) hog, pig.

example:
Daniela era **tunca**, pero después de estar a régimen seis meses, está guapísima.

translation:
Daniela used to be **fat**, but after dieting for six months, she's beautiful.

vaca f. fatso (applies only to a woman) • (lit.): cow.

example:
¡Este vestido me hace parecer como una **vaca**!

translation:
This dress makes me look like a **fat cow**!

Jerk / Idiot • Crazy / Stupid

adoquín adj. (Cuba)
• (lit.): paving stone.

example:
Carlos es tan **adoquín**. Echó agua accidentalmente en el depósito de gasolina y ¡estropeó su coche!

translation:
Carlos is such an **idiot**. He accidentally put water in his gas tank and ruined his car!

baboso/a n. & adj. • idiot; stupid (lit.): one who dribbles a lot.

example:
Victor llegó tarde su primer día
de trabajo porque se le olvidó
la dirección. ¡Qué **baboso**!

translation:
Victor was late his first day on
the job because he forgot the
address. What an **idiot**!

bereco/a n. & adj. (El Savador)
idiot; stupid.

example:
Angélica es tan **bereca**. Echó
sal en el café pensando que
era azucar.

translation:
Angelica is so **stupid**. She put
salt in her coffee thinking it
was sugar.

bobo/a n. & adj. idiot; stupid
• (lit.): foolish.

example:
Luis es **bobo** si piensa que le
voy a prestar más dinero.

translation:
Luis is **crazy** if he thinks he
can borrow more money from
me!

bofa n. (Cuba).

example:
Mira a esa **bofa**. Está
hablando sola.

translation:
Look at that **crazy
woman**. She's talking to
herself.

NOTE: This is from the verb
bofarse meaning "to sag."

bonachón/na n. & adj.
sucker, simpleton; gullible
• (lit.): someone who is too
nice and good (from the
adjective *bueno* meaning
"good").

example:
Enrique se cree todo lo que
le dices. ¡Es un **buenón**!

translation:
Enrique believes everything
you tell him. What a
sucker!

buche n. & adj. (Cuba) idiot;
crazy • (lit.): mouthful.

example:
Si fuera tú, no me fiaría de
él. Francamente, creo que
está un poco **buche**.

translation:
I wouldn't trust him if I were
you. Frankly, I think he's a
little **crazy**.

buey m. & adj. idiot; stupid
• (lit.): ox, bullock.

example:
A Juan se le olvidó ponerse los pantalones para salir. ¡Qué **buey**!

translation:
Juan forgot to put on his pants when he went outside. What a **geek**!

burro/a n. & adj. jerk; crazy.
• (lit.): donkey.

example:
¡Nunca saldría con un **burro** como ese!

translation:
I'd never go out with a **jerk** like that!

NOTE: In Mexico, the term **burro/a** is also used to mean "a bad student."

cebollín m. (Cuba) stupid person • (lit.): small onion.

example:
Me pregunto cómo un **cebollín** como Oscar ha podido sacar una A en el examen de matemáticas.

translation:
I wonder how an **idiot** like Oscar got an A on the math test!

cebollón m. (Cuba) stupid person • (lit.): large onion.

example:
Todo el mundo piensa que Marcelo es un **cebollón**, pero la verdad es que es un genio.

translation:
Everyone thinks that Marcelo is an **idiot**, but he's actually a genius.

chiflado/a n. & adj. crackpot; crazy, nuts • (lit.): whistled (from the verb *chiflar* meaning "to whistle").

example:
Si crees que puedes conducir de San Francisco a Los Angeles en sólo tres horas, ¡estás **chiflado**!

translation:
If you think you can drive to Los Angeles from San Francisco in only three hours, you're **nuts**!

chirusa f. (Argentina) idiotic little girl • (lit.): ignorant young woman.

example:
¿Conociste a la hija de Marcela? ¡Qué **chirusa**!

translation:
Did you meet Marcela's daughter? What a little **geek**!

comebasura *n. & adj.* idiot;
stupid • (lit.): garbage-eater.

example:
Alfredo es un verdadero
comebasura. Le dice a todo
el mundo que pertenece a la
realeza.

translation:
Alfredo is a real **idiot**. He tells
everyone that he is royalty.

corto/a de mate *adj.*
(Argentina) • (lit.): short in the
gourd.

example:
Creo que nuestra profesora es
un poco **corta de mate**. En
sus clases se empieza a reir sin
motivo.

translation:
I think our new teacher is a
little **touched in the head**.
During her lectures, she starts
laughing for no reason.

cretinita *f. & adj. (Argentina)*
idiotic little girl; jerky
• (lit.): little cretin.

example:
¡Esa **cretinita** me ha robado
el bolígrafo!

translation:
That **little cretin** stole my
pen!

cretino *m. & adj.* jerk; jerky
• (lit.): cretin.

example:
El hermano de Steve es un
pequeño **cretino**. No para
de desatarme los cordones
de mis zapatos.

translation:
Steve's brother is a little
cretin. He keeps untying
my shoes.

guabina *f. (Cuba).*

example:
¡Qué **guabina**! Paula está
todo el día tirada viendo la
televisión.

translation:
What an **idiot**! Paula just
sits around and watches
television all day.

guaje *m. & adj. (El Salvador,
Mexico)* idiot; stupid.

example:
¿Has visto el sombrero que
lleva Pancho? Le hace
parecer **guaje**.

translation:
Did you see the hat Pancho
is wearing? It makes him
look like a **jerk**.

hecho polvo *exp. (Spain)*
• (lit.): made of dust.

example:
Arnaldo parece un **hecho
polvo** con sus gafas
nuevas.

translation:
Arnaldo looks like a **geek** in his new glasses.

NOTE: In Mexico, this expression is used to mean "to ache." For example: *Mis pies están hechos polvo*; My feet are aching.

latoso/a *n. & adj.* jerk, pain-in-the-neck; jerky. • (lit.): made of tin can.

example:
Simón es un **latoso**. Me sigue a todas partes.

translation:
Simón is an **annoying little jerk**. He follows me around everywhere.

locote *n.* big idiot.

example:
Mi hermana es psiquiatra y trabaja con **locotes** todo el día.

translation:
My sister is a psychiatrist who works with **crazy people** all day long.

NOTE: This is from the adjective *loco/a* meaning "crazy."

lurio/a *adj. (Mexico)*
• (lit.): mad, crazy.

example:
Si te crees que te puedes comer esa tarta entera, tú estás **lurio**.

translation:
If you think you can eat that entire cake, you're **crazy**.

VARIATION: **lurias** *adj.*

maje *adj.* crazy.

example:
Tú estás **maje** si crees que el jefe te va a conceder un ascenso.

translation:
You're **out of your mind** if you think the boss is going to give you a raise.

NOTE: This is from the verb *majar* meaning "to crush, pound, mash."

menso/a *(Mexico) n. & adj.* idiot; jerky • (lit.): foolish, stupid.

example:
Acabo de enterarme de que Carla está en un hospital psiquiátrico. No sabía que estaba **mensa**.

translation:
I just heard that Carla is in a mental hospital. I didn't know she was **nuts**.

necio/a *n. & adj.* fool; foolish • (lit.): foolish.

example:
La gente que no practica el sexo de forma segura es una **necia**.

translation:
People who don't practice safe sex are **crazy**.

papo/a *n. & adj. (El Salvador)* idiot; crazy.

example:
Jaime es un **papo** si piensa que va ser médico algún día. No es lo suficientemente listo.

translation:
Jaime is a **nut** if he thinks he's going to be a doctor someday. He's not smart enough.

pelmazo/a *n.* • (lit.): undigested food.

example:
¡Ese **pelmazo** se ha saltado un semáforo en rojo!

translation:
That **idiot** ran a red light!

pelota *n. & adj.* idiot; stupid.

example:
¡Marco es tan **pelota**! ¡El manejó en la calle en sentido contrario!

translation:
Marco is such an **idiot**! He drove down the street in the wrong direction!

pelotudo/a *n. & adj.* idiot; stupid.

example:
Se me ha olvidado mi cita con el médico. ¡Qué **pelotudo**!

translation:
I forgot about my doctor's appointment. What an **idiot**!

NOTE: This is from the feminine noun *pelota* meaning "ball."

rayado/a *n. & adj.* idiot; stupid *(Argentina)*
• (lit.): striped one.

example:
Laura no sabe cómo encender su computadora. Está **rayada**.

translation:
Laura can't figure out how to turn on her computer. She's **stupid**.

safado/a *n. & adj.* idiot, fool; foolish • (lit.): brazen, bold.

example:
Mi nuevo jefe no deja de hablar solo. ¡Está **safado**!

translation:
My new boss keeps talking to himself all the time. He's a **real idiot**!

socotroco/a *n. & adj. (Cuba)* idiot; stupid.

example:
¿Por qué quieres salir con Ernesto? Es todo un **socotroco**. ¡Ni siquiera sabe cuánto son dos más dos!

translation:
Why do you want to go out with Ernesto? He's such an **idiot**. He can't even add two plus two!

soreco/a *n. & adj.* idiot; stupid *(El Salvador)*.

example:
Soy tan **soreca**. No puedo descilrar cómo componer mi nueva bicicleta.

translation:
I'm so **stupid**. I just can't figure out how to assemble my new bicycle.

tapado/a *n. & adj.* idiot; stupid • (lit.): covered-up.

example:
Mi nueva vecina sale a la calle en bañador en pleno invierno. Creo que está un poco **tapada**.

translation:
My new neighbor wears bathing suits outside during the winter. I think she's a little **nuts**.

tarado/a *n. & adj.* idiot; stupid. • (lit.): defective, damaged.

example:
Si te crees que me voy a levantar tan pronto para llevarte al aeropuerto, ¡estás **tarado**! Vete en taxi.

translation:
If you think I'm going to get up that early to drive you to the airport, you're **nuts**! Just take a taxi.

tarugo/a *n. & adj. (Guatemala, Mexico)* idiot; stupid • (lit.): wooden peg.

example:
Creía que mi novio era normal. Pero después de unos meses me dí cuenta de que es un **tarugo**.

translation:
I thought my boyfriend was so normal. But after a few months, I realized that he's really a **crackpot**!

totoreco/a *n. & adj. (El Salvador)* idiot; stupid • (lit.): stunned, confused, bewildered.

example:
¡Quítate la pantalla de la lámpara de la cabeza! ¡La gente va a pensar que estás **totoreco**!

translation:
Take that lamp shade off your head! People are you going to think you're **crazy**!

zopenco/a *n. & adj.* jerk; stupid • (lit.): dull, stupid.

example:
¡Nunca saldría con Jorge! ¡Es un **zopenco**!

translation:
I'd never go out with Jorge! He's such a **jerk**!

Lazy

aplomado/a *n. & adj.* lazy bum; lazy • (lit.): serious, solemn.

example:
Miguel nunca se ofrecerá a ayudarte. Es demasiado **aplomado**.

translation:
Miguel will never volunteer to help you. He's so **lazy**.

aragán *n. & adj.* lazy bum; lazy.

example:
Nunca he conocido a nadie tan **aragán** como Pedro. Está durmiendo todo el día.

translation:
I've never met anyone as **lazy** as Pedro. All he does is sleep all day.

arrastrado/a *n. & adj.* lazy bum; lazy. • (lit.): wretched, miserable.

example:
Angela y yo hicimos una gran fiesta, pero no me ayudó nada. ¡Es tan **arrastrada**!

translation:
Angela and I threw a big party, but she didn't help me at all. She's so **lazy**!

bacán *m. (Argentina, Uruguay)* lazy bum.

example:
¡Eres un **bacán**! ¡Levántate del sofá y ponte a trabajar!

translation:
You're such a **lazy bum**! Get off the couch and do some work!

¡Ché dejá de dormir, fiaca de mierda, movéte un poco! *exp.* (Argentina) used in response to seeing a lazy person • (lit.): Hey, stop sleeping, you lazy piece of shit, and move around a little!

example:
¡Ché dejá de dormir, fiaca de mierda, movéte un poco! ¡Tenemos mucho trabajo que hacer!

translation:
Hey, stop sleeping, you lazy piece of shit, and move around a little! We have a lot of work to do!

conchudo/a n. & adj. lazy bum; lazy.

example:
Mi hermano es tan **conchudo**. El no hace nada todo el día.

translation:
My brother is so **lazy**. He doesn't do a thing all day.

dormilón/ona n. & adj. lazy bum; lazy • (lit.): one who sleeps a lot (from the verb dormir meaning "to sleep").

example:
Mi invitado es un **dormilón**. Está todo el día durmiendo.

translation:
My house guest is such a **lazy bum**. All he does is sleep all day.

empollón/ona n. & adj. lazy bum; lazy • (lit.): grind.

example:
Mi jefe es tan **empollón**, que al final termino haciendo yo todo el trabajo.

translation:
My boss is so **lazy** that I end up doing all of his work!

flojo/a n. & adj. lazy bum; lazy • (lit.): loose, weak.

example:
Eres demasiado **flojo**. Tienes que intentar motivarte.

translation:
You're so **lazy**. You need to try and get motivated.

follón/ona n. & adj. lazy bum; lazy.

example:
Tienes que dejar de ser un **follón** o nunca encotrarás trabajo.

translation:
You've got to stop being such a **lazy bum** or you'll never find a job.

gafitas m. (Spain) • (lit.): small eyeglasses.

example:
He decidido echar a Adolfo. Es buen chico pero es un **gafitas**.

translation:
I've decided to fire Adolfo.
He's a very good guy but
he's a **lazy bum**.

gandul/a *n. & adj.* lazy bum;
lazy.

example:
La razón por la que se está
hundiendo esta compañía es
porque hay demasiados
gandules en ella.

translation:
The reason this company isn't
surviving is because there are
too many **lazy people** in it.

grandote boludo *m.*
(*Argentina*) big lazy bum
• (lit.): big-balled (testicles)
one.

example:
Mi abuelo es un **grandote
boludo**. Está todo el día
bebiendo cerveza y viendo la
televisión.

translation:
My grandfather is such a **lazy
bum**. He drinks beer and
watches television all day.

holgazán/ana *n. & adj.* lazy
bum; lazy • (lit.): lazy, indolent.

example:
Odio esta camisa. Me hace
parecer un **holgazán**.

translation:
I hate this shirt. It makes me
look like a **geek**.

huevón/ona (ser un) *n. &
adj.* lazy bum; lazy • (lit.): to
be like a testicle (since
huevón comes from the term
huevo which literally means
"egg" but it used in slang to
mean "testicle").

example:
Mi hermano y yo somos
completamente opuestos.
Yo soy muy activo y él es un
huevón.

translation:
My brother and I are totally
opposite. I'm very motivated
and he's a **lazy bum**.

perezoso/a *n. & adj.* lazy
bum; lazy • (lit.): [same].

example:
Laura vino a mi casa para
ayudarme a cocinar para la
fiesta, pero yo hice casi todo
el trabajo. No sabía que era
tan **perezosa**.

translation:
Laura came over to my
house to help me cook for
our party, but I did most of
the work. I didn't realize she
was so **lazy**.

Not to give a damn

no importar un carajo *exp.*
- (lit.): not to mind a penis.

example:
Jorge **no me importa un carajo**. Ya no somos amigos.

translation:
I **don't give a damn** about Jorge. We're not friends any more.

no importar un cojón *exp.*
- (lit.): not to care a testicle.

example:
A Beatriz **no le importan un cojón** sus clases. Por eso está suspendiendolo todo.

translation:
Beatriz **doesn't give a damn** about her school work. That's why she's failing all of her classes.

no importar un huevo *exp.*
- (lit.): egg (or "testicle").

example:
A Daniel no le importa un huevo su trabajo. Sinceramente, creo que le van a echar pronto.

translation:
Daniel doesn't give a damn about his job. Frankly, I think he's going to get fired soon.

no importar un pepino
exp. • (lit.): not to care a cucumber.

example:
No me importa un pepino lo que la gente piense de mí.

translation:
I don't give a damn what people think about me.

Pain-in-the-neck / Annoying person

corcho *m. (El Salvador)* annoying person or idiot
- (lit.): cork.

example:
Guillermo me sigue a todas partes. ¡Es un **corcho**!

translation:
Guillermo follows me everywhere. He's such a **pain-in-the-neck**!

estorbo *m.* • (lit.): obstacle.

example:
Cada vez que doy mi opinión sobre algo, Oscar discute con migo. Es un **estorbo**.

translation:
Every time I give an opinion about something, Oscar argues with me. He's such a **pain-in-the-neck**!

fregado/a *n. & adj.* annoying person, pain-in-the-neck; annoying • (lit.): scrubbing.

example:
Jaime es un **fregado**. ¡Me llama por teléfono cinco veces al día!

translation:
Jaime is such a **pain-in-the-neck**. He calls me on the telephone five times a day!

fregón/ona *n. & adj.* pain-in-the-neck; annoying • (lit.): one who scrubs.

example:
Victor es un **fregón**. Cada vez que hablamos no hace más que contarme problemas.

translation:
Victor is a **pain-in-the-neck**. Every time we talk, he does nothing but tell me about his problems.

NOTE: This term is also commonly used to describe someone who is extremely impressive and "cool."

hinchapelotas *m.*
• (lit.): one who makes someone's testicles swell.

example:
No puedo aguantar a Marco. Es un **hinchapelotas**. ¡Usa mis cosas sin pedírmelas!

translation:
I can't stand Marco. He's a **pain-in-the-neck**. He borrows my things without asking!

NOTE: **pelotas** *f.pl.* testicles • (lit.): balls (in a game).

latoso/a *n. & adj.* pain-in-the-neck; annoying person • (lit.): made of tin can.

example:
Diana es una **latosa**. No hace más que pedirme favores.

translation:
Diana is a **pain-in-the-neck**. All she ever does is ask me for favors.

Runt

chaparro/a *n. & adj.* runt; runty.

example:
¡Hey **chaparro**! ¡Muevete!

translation:
Hey, **shorty**! Move it!

corchito m. (*Argentina*) • (lit.): little cork.

example:
El **corchito** de Joseph me pidió salir el sábado por la noche.

translation:
That **little runt** Joseph asked me out on Saturday night.

enano/a n. & adj. runt; runty. • (lit.): dwarf.

example:
John se cree que es un tipo duro, pero no es más que un **enano**.

translation:
John thinks he's so tough but he's nothing but a **little runt**.

inspector de zócalo m. (*Argentina*) • (lit.): baseboard inspector.

example:
¿Le pediste a Enrique que te ayudara a mover el piano? ¡Pero si es un **inspector de zócalo**!

translation:
You asked Enrique to help you move your piano? But he's such a **little runt**!

mierdecilla f. • (lit.) small shit.

example:
Ese **mierdecilla** es un presuntuoso y ni siquiera le gusta a nadie.

translation:
That **little runt** acts so conceited but no one even likes him.

petiso de mierda m. (*Argentina*) • (lit.): little shit.

example:
No voy a invitar a ese **petiso de mierda** a mi fiesta de cumpleaños.

translation:
I'm not going to invite that **little shit** to my birthday party.

poca cosa f. & adj. runt; runty • (lit.): little thing.

example:
Mi hermana sale con un **poca cosa**. ¡Están ridículos juntos, porque ella es tan alta!

translation:
My sister is dating a **little runt**. They look ridiculous together because my sister is so tall!

Scaredy-cat / Coward

coyón/na *n. & adj.* scaredy-cat; scared.

example:
¡Soy demasiado **coyón** para tirarme en paracaídas!

translation:
I'm too much of a **scaredy-cat** to try parachuting!

sacatón/ona *n. & adj.* scaredy-cat; scared • (lit.): from the verb *sacar* meaning "to pull away quickly."

example:
Simón no sale por la noche. Es un **sacatón**.

translation:
Simón won't go outside at night. He's a **scaredy-cat**.

Showoff (to be a)

farolero/a (ser un/a) *n. & adj.* showoff; showy • (lit.): lantern maker.

example:
Nancy es una **farolera**. Yo creo que le gusta llamar la atención.

translation:
Nancy is such a **showoff**. I think she likes a lot of attention.

ostentador/a *n. & adj.* showoff; showy • (lit.): one who is ostentatious.

example:
¿Has visto lo que llevaba Claudia puesto? ¡Qué **ostentadora**!

translation:
Did you see what Claudia was wearing? What a **showoff**!

Shut up!

¡Cállate! *interj.* • (lit.): Shut yourself!

example:
¡**Cállate**! ¡Hablas demasiado!

translation:
Shut up! You talk too much!

¡Cállate/Cierra el hocico! *interj.* • (lit.): Shut your mouth!

example:
¡**Cállate/Cierra el hocico**! ¡Es mentira!

translation:
Shut up! That's a lie!

NOTE: hocico *m.* • (lit.): the mouth of an animal (and derogatory when used in reference to a person).

¡Cállate/Cierra el pico! *exp.*
Shut your trap! • (lit.): Shut
your beak!

example:
¡Cállate/Cierra el pico!
¡Lo que estás diciendo es
mentira!

translation:
Shut your trap! What
you're saying is a lie!

¡Cállate/Cierra la boca! *exp.*
• (lit.): Close your mouth!

example:
¡Cállate/Cierra la boca!
¡Deja de hablar de ella de ese
modo!

translation:
Shut your mouth! Stop
talking about her that way!

Snob(by)

alzado/a *n. & adj.* snob; stuck
up • (lit.): from the verb *alzar*
meaning "to lift" which refers
to a snobby person's nose in
the air.

example:
¡Diana es tan **alzada**! Sólo
va a restaurantes caros.

translation:
Diana is so **snobby**! She only
goes to expensive restaurants.

ampuloso/a *n. & adj.* snob;
stuck up • (lit.): verbose,
pompous, full of
redundancies.

example:
Laura es una **ampulosa**.
Sólo invita a gente rica a sus
fiestas.

translation:
Laura is a **snob**. She only
invites rich people to her
parties.

cuello duro *m. & adj.* snob;
stuck up • (lit.): hard or stiff
neck (from keeping one's
nose in the air).

example:
Miguel es un **cuello duro**.
Sólo viaja en primera clase.

translation:
Miguel is a **snob**. He'll only
travel first class.

fufú *m. & adj.* snob; stuck up
• (lit.): Cuban dish made of
plantain & pork rind.

example:
Desde que Arnaldo se hizo
rico, se ha convertido en un
fufú.

translation:
Ever since Arnaldo became
rich, he's become a **snob**.

fufurufu *n. & adj.* snob; stuck up.

example:
Mi tio es millonario pero no es un **fufurufu** para nada. Tiene los pies en la tierra.

translation:
My uncle is a millionaire but he's not a **snob** at all. He's very down-to-earth.

lleno/a de humos *adj.* (*Argentina*) • (lit.): full of smoke.

example:
La tía de David está **llena de humos**. Se niega a hablar con la gente que no es rica.

translation:
David's aunt is **very snobby**. She refuses to speak to people who aren't rich.

Stingy

aceite *n. & adj.* (*Cuba*) tightwad; stingy • (lit.): oil.

example:
Eres tan **aceite**. Nunca te ofreces a pagar la cena.

translation:
You're so **stingy**. You never offer to pay for dinner.

agarrado/a *n. & adj.* tightwad; stingy • (lit.): held.

example:
Antonio es muy **agarrado**. Nunca le compra regalos a nadie.

translation:
Antonio is very **stingy**. He never buys people gifts.

apretado/a *n. & adj.* (*Mexico*) tightwad; stingy • (lit.): squashed, tightly- packed.

example:
Angela solía ser muy **apretada**. Pero desde que le ha tocado la lotería, se ha vuelto muy generosa.

translation:
Angela used to be very **stingy**. But now that she won the lottery, she's become very generous.

codo *m. & adj.* tightwad; stingy • (lit.): elbow.

example:
La razón por la que mi tío es tan rico es porque es un **codo**. Nunca se gasta dinero en nada.

translation:
The reason my uncle is so rich is because he's a **tightwad**. He never spends money on anything.

mendigo/a *n. & adj.* tightwad; stingy • (lit.): beggar, mendicant.

example:
¿Te puedes creer el regalo tan barato que me hizo Geraldo para mi cumpleaños? ¡Qué **mendigo**!

translation:
Can you believe the cheap gift Geraldo gave me for my birthday? What a **cheap-skate**!

pichicato/a n. & adj. tightwad; stingy.

example:
¿Quieres que andemos diez millas? No seas **pichicato**. Vamos a coger un taxi.

translation:
You want us to walk ten miles? Don't be such a **cheapskate**. Let's just get a taxi.

Stink (to)

apestar v. • (lit.): to infect with the plague.

example:
¡Esta tienda de perfumes **apesta**!

translation:
This perfume shop **stinks to high heaven**!

ALSO: **peste** f. stink, foul smell • (lit.): plague, epidemic disease • *¡Qué peste!;* What a horrible smell!

Ugly / Ugly person

cáncamo m. *(Cuba)*
• (lit.): louse.

example:
¡Qué **cáncamo**! Me pregunto cómo puede tener una hermana tan guapa.

translation:
What an **ugly man**! I wonder how he could have such a beautiful sister!

casco m. ugly woman • (lit.): helmet.

example:
Paula era un **casco**, pero despues de la cirujía estética, está guapísima.

translation:
Paula used to be a **real ugly woman**, but after her plastic surgery, she's beautiful.

cotunto/a adj. *(Cuba)*.

example:
¿Viste el traje que llevaba Antonina en la fiesta? Era **contunto**.

translation:
Did you see that dress Antonina was wearing at the party? It was **so ugly**.

LECCIÓN TRES - Vulgar Insults & Name-Calling

¡Qué perra!
¡Cási destruyó mi carro!

*(trans.): What a **bitch**! She almost destroyed my car!*
*(lit.): What a **female dog**! She almost destroyed my car!*

Lección Tres · Dialogue in Slang

Sergio: ¡Mira a esa **jodida pendeja**!

Magda: ¿**Qué coño está haciendo**? ¡Qué **ojete**! ¿Es que no sabes manejar?

Juan: ¡**Maldita puta**! Debe **tener la regla**.

Magda: ¡**Gilipollas**! ¡Odio a los **chupa vergas** como tú! ¡**Me cago en tu puta madre**!

Sergio: ¡**Métete el dedo en el culo**!

Juan: ¡Qué **perra**!

Sergio: Casi destruye mi automóvil y todavía se enoja. ¡**Vete al cuerno**!

Magda: ¡**Hijo de puta**!

Sergio: ¡**Lameculos**!

Magda: ¡**Maricón**!

Juan: Sergio, déjala en paz. Ya nos tenemos que ir. Vamos a llegar tarde al Seminario.

What a bitch! She almost destroyed my car!

Sergio: Look at that **fucking bitch**!

Magda: **What the hell are you doing**? What an **asshole**! Don't you know how to drive?

Juan: What a **fucking whore**! She must be **on the rag.**

Magda: **Bastard**! I can't stand **cocksuckers** like you! **Fuck you**!

Sergio: **Shove it up your ass**!

Juan: What a **bitch**!

Sergio: She almost destroys my car and she's mad at me. **Go to hell**!

Magda: **Son of a whore**!

Sergio: **Ass licker**!

Magda: **Faggot**!

Juan: Sergio, forget about her. We need to get going. We only have five more minutes before we're late for seminary school.

Vocabulary

chupa vergas *n. & adj.* asshole, cocksucker; jerky • (lit.): penis sucker.

example:
Juan no me devolvió el dinero que le presté. ¡Qué **chupa vergas**!

translation:
Juan never returned the money he borrowed from me. What a **cocksucker**!

NOTE: The feminine noun *verga* is typically used in reference to the penis of an animal.

gilipollas *n. & adj.* *(Spain)* bastard; fucked (of a contemptible person) • (lit.): stupid dick.

example:
Ricardo es un **gilipollas**. Siempre me está diciendo mentiras.

translation:
Ricardo is a **bastard**. He's always telling me lies.

hijo de puta *m.* son of a bitch • (lit.): son of a whore.

example:
Ese **hijo de puta** intentó timarme.

translation:
That **son of a bitch** tried to rip me off.

VARIATION -1: hijo de su puta madre • (lit.): son of one's whore mother.

VARIATION -2: hijo puta • (lit.): son whore.

jodida/pinche pendeja *f.* fucking bitch, fucking idiot • (lit.): fucking fool.

example:
¡**Jodida/Pinche pendeja**! Esta mujer no sabe ni freir un huevo.

translation:
Fucking idiot! This woman doesn't even know how to fry an egg.

NOTE -1: In Spain, the adjective *jodida* would be used in this expression, whereas in Mexico, the commonly used adjective would be *pinche*.

NOTE -2: If the above expression were to be used in the masculine form *(¡Jodido pendejo!)*, the translation would be "Fucking looser!"

SYNONYM: **jodida/pinche puta** *f.* • (lit.): fucking whore.

¡Me cago en tu puta madre! *interj.* Fuck you! • (lit.): I shit in your whore mother!

example:
¡Me cago en tu puta madre! ¡No te quiero ver más!

translation:
Fuck you! I don't want to see you any more!

SYNONYM: **¡Me cago en la madre que te parió!** *interj.* • (lit.): I shit on the mother who gave you birth!

lameculos *n.* ass-licker • (lit.): [same].

example:
Ernesto es un **lameculos**. Deberías de ver cómo se porta cuando está con el jefe.

translation:
Ernesto is an **ass-licker**. You should see the way he behaves with the boss.

maldita puta *f.* (used in contempt) fucking whore • (lit.): damned whore.

example:
¡Maldita puta! Rosalinda es una mentirosa.

translation:
Fucking whore! Rosalinda is a liar.

maricón *m. & adj.* fag; faggy • (lit.): faggot, homosexual.

example:
Llamar a un homosexual, **maricón**, es muy despectivo.

translation:
Calling a homosexual a **fag** is very derogatory.

SYNONYM: **marica** *m.* • (lit.): homosexual.

¡Métete el dedo en el culo! *exp.* Shove it up your ass! • (lit.): Put your finger up your ass!

example:
¿Quieres que te preste dinero por la tercera vez esta semana? **¡Métete el dedo en el culo!**

translation:
You want me to lend you money for the third time this week? **Shove it up your ass!**

ojete *m.* asshole • (lit.): large eye.

example:
¿Vas a invitar a Manuel a tu casa? ¡Es un verdadero **ojete**!

translation:
You're going to invite Manuel to your house? He's such an **asshole**!

perra *f.* bitch • (lit.): bitch, female dog.

example:
Esa tipa es una **perra**. Siempre está de mal humor.

translation:
That girl is a **bitch**. She is always in a bad mood.

tener la regla *exp.* to be menstruating, "to be on the rag" • (lit.): to have the rule.

example:
Verónica está de muy mal humor hoy. Debe **tener la regla**.

translation:
Veronica is in a very bad mood today. She must **be on the rag**.

SYNONYM: **de trapitos (estar)** • (lit.): to be on little rags.

¿Qué coño estás haciendo? *interj*. What the hell are you doing? • (lit.): What the cunt are you doing?

example:
¿Qué coño estás haciendo? ¡No quiero que hagas eso otra vez!

translation:
What the hell are you doing? I don't want you to do that again!

NOTE: In Mexico, *coño* is replaced by *carajo*. The noun *coño* is very common in Spain and Cuba.

¡Vete al cuerno! *interj*. Go to hell! • (lit.): Go to the horn (of animals)!

example:
¡Vete al cuerno! ¡No vuelvas por aquí nunca más!

translation:
Go to hell! Don't you ever come back here again!

A CLOSER LOOK:
Vulgar Insults and Name-Calling

It seems that one of the best ways to learn offensive name-calling is to hop in a cab, sit back, and just listen. Within minutes, you will have heard some of the most "earthy" words and imaginative expressions soar out of the cabby's mouth. Since I've gotten into the habit of carrying a pen and paper with me wherever I go, over the years I've managed to pick up some very colorful and commonly used terms guaranteed to make any visitor fit right in.

¡A la puñeta! *interj.* *(Cuba)* Go to hell! • (lit.): Go to masturbation!

example:
La próxima vez que me insulte Olivia, ¡la voy a mandar **a la puñeta**!

translation:
The next time Olivia insults me, I'm going to tell her **to go to hell**!

¡A la verga! *intjer.* Fuck it! • (lit.): To the penis!

example:
¡**A la verga**! Este trabajo es demasiado difícil.

translation:
Fuck it! This job is too difficult.

asqueroso/a *n. & adj.* jerk, disgusting person; jerky • (lit.): filthy.

example:
John es un **asqueroso**; no me gusta nada.

translation:
John is such a **jerk**. I really don't like him.

¡Ay que la chingada! *interj.* Oh, shit!

example:
¡**Ay que la chingada**! ¡Me he dejado las llaves dentro del coche!

translation:
Oh, shit! I locked my keys in the car!

besa mi culo *exp.* kiss my ass.

example:
Si el jefe quiere que trabaje hasta tarde hoy también, puede **besarme el culo**.

translation:
If the boss wants me to work late again, he can **kiss my ass**.

VARIATION: bésame el culo *exp.*

cabrón/ona *n. & adj.* asshole; jerky • (lit.): billy-goat.

example:
¡Ese **cabrón** me robó la novia!

translation:
That **bastard** stole my girlfriend!

VARIATION: re-cabrón *m.* *(Argentina)* a big asshole.

NOTE: In Argentina, the prefix *re-* is commonly added to many words to add greater emphasis.

¡Cago en tu leche! *interj.* Fuck you! • (lit.): I shit in your milk!

example:
¡Como te atreves a decirme eso! **¡Cago en tu leche**!

translation:
How dare you say that to me! **Fuck you**!

calientapollas *n. & adj.* (Spain) prick teaser • (lit.): one who makes a penis (*polla*, literally "young chicken") hot (*caliente*).

example:
Marta es una **calientapollas**.

translation:
Marta is such a **prick teaser**.

capullo *m.* bastard, asshole • (lit.): bud or head of the penis.

example:
Adolfo es un **capullo**. Siempre miente.

translation:
Adolfo is a **bastard**. He lies all the time.

¡Chúpamela! *interj.* Suck my dick! • (lit.): Suck it!

¡Chúpa mi pinga! *interj.* Suck my dick! • (lit.): [same].

¡Chúpa mi polla! *interj.* Suck my dick! • (lit.): Suck my young chicken!

¡Chúpa mi verga! *interj.* Suck my dick! • (lit.): Suck my penis (of an animal).

¡Chúpame, puto! *interj.* Suck my dick, you asshole! Fuck you! • (lit.): Suck me, you faggot!

¡Chíngate! *interj.* (Mexico) Fuck you! (from the verb *chingar* meaning "to fuck").

¡Chinga tu madre! *interj.* • (lit.): Fuck your mother!

chingón *m.* fucker (from the verb *chingar* meaning "to fuck").

example:
¡Nunca confiaré en un **chingón** como Oliver!

translation:
I would never trust a **fucker** like Oliver!

NOTE: This term is also commonly used to describe someone who is extremely impressive and "fucking cool."

cojudo/a *n. & adj.* idiot; stupid • (lit.): uncastrated.

example:
Clara es **cojuda**. Se cree todo
lo que le dicen.

translation:
Clara is **really gullible**. She
believes anything you tell her.

comemierda n. & adj. jerk;
jerky • (lit.): shit-eater.

example:
Marcelo es un **comemierda**.
No creo que nunca se case.

translation:
Marcelo is such an **idiot**.
I don't think he'll ever be able
to get married.

**como bocina de avión
(estar/ser)** exp. (Argentina)
to be as useless as a screen
door on a submarine • (lit.): to
be like a horn in a plane.

example:
No te va a poder ayudar.
**Está como una bocina
de avión**.

translation:
He's not going to be able to
help you. **He's as useless as
a screen door on a sub-
marine**.

VARIATION: inútil como
bocina de avión
(estar/ser) exp. • (lit.): useless as a horn in a plane.

**como un cenicero de
moto (estar/ser)** exp.
(Argentina) to be totally
useless • (lit.): to be like an
ashtray on a motorcycle.

example:
No te voy a poder ayudar
con la tarea. Cuando se
trata de matemáticas soy
**como un cenicero de
moto**.

translation:
I'm not going to be able to
help you with your home-
work. When it comes to
math, I'm as **useless as a
screen door on a sub-
marine**.

VARIATION: inútil como
un cenicero de moto
(estar/ser) exp. • (lit.): to
be as useless as an ashtray
on a motorcycle.

cutre n. & adj. idiot; stupid.

example:
Diego es un **cutre**. Nos dijo
que nos invitaba a cenar y
después pagó sólo su
comida.

translation:
Diego is so **cheap**. He told
us he was treating us for
dinner, but only paid for his
own food.

NOTE: When said of a person, *cutre* means "cheap" or "bad taste." When said of a place, it means "dirty, old, & ugly."

denso/a *n. & adj. (Argentina)* pain-in-the-neck; annoying • (lit.): dense.

example:
Ahí está Dennis. Espero que no venga y me empiece a hablar. ¡Es tan **denso**!

translation:
There's Dennis. I hope he doesn't come over here and start talking to me. He's so **annoying**!

gilipollas *m. (Spain)* idiot, jerk • (lit.): stupid dick.

example:
No te creas nada de lo que te diga ese **gilipollas**. Es un mentiroso.

translation:
Don't believe anything that **jerk** tells you. He's a big liar.

gordo/a como una ballena *exp.* • (lit.): as fat as a whale an elephant.

example:
Si te comes la tarta entera, te vas a poner **gordo como una ballena**.

translation:
If you eat that entire cake, you're going to be as **fat as a pig**.

VARIATION: **gordo/a como un elefante** *adj.* • (lit.): fat as an elephant.

guey *m. & adj.* jerk, idiot; jerky • (lit.): variation of *buey* meaning "ox" or "bullock."

example:
No me puedo creer que salgas con Antonio; ¡es un **guey**!

translation:
I can't believe you're going out with Antonio. He's such a **jerk**!

¡Hijo de tu chingada madre! *interj.* You son of a bitch! • (lit.): Son of your fucking mother!

example:
¡Me has estropeado mi bicicleta nueva! **¡Hijo de tu chingada madre**!

translation:
You ruined my new bicycle! **You son of a bitch**!

¡Hostia puta! *interj.* Holy shit! • (lit.): Fucking sacred wafer!

example:
¡Hostia puta! ¡Mira cómo
llueve!

translation:
Holy Shit! Look at all that
rain!

¡Jódete y aprieta el culo!
exp. (Cuba) Go fuck yourself!
• (lit.): Fuck you and hold your
ass tight!

example:
¡Me has engañado! **¡Jódete y
aprieta el culo**!

translation:
You cheated me! **Go fuck
yourself**!

jodida/pinche puta *f.* fucking
bitch • (lit.): fucking whore.

example:
¡Ésa **jodida/pinche puta**
me ha zancadilleado!

translation:
That **fucking bitch** tripped
me!

NOTE: In Spain, the adjective
jodida would be used in this
expression, whereas in Mexico,
the commonly used adjective
would be *pinche*.

¡La puta que te parió! *interj.*
You son of a bitch! • (lit.): The
whore that gave you birth!

example:
¿Cómo has podido hacer
algo tan horrible? **¡La puta
que te parió**!

translation:
How could you do such a
horrible thing? **You son of
a bitch**!

lagartona *f.* • **1.** prostitute,
whore • **2.** bitch • (lit.): big
lizard.

example:
Karen se acuesta con todos.
¡Estoy empezando a pensar
que es una **lagarta**!

translation:
Karen has sex with every-
body. I am starting to think
she's a **whore**!

lambiscón/ona *n. & adj.*
brown-noser.

example:
Eduardo Haskell es muy
cumplido con mi madre; es
un **lambiscón**.

translation:
Eduardo Haskell always
gives my mother compli-
ments. He's such a
brown-noser

lameculos *m.* brown-noser
• (lit.): ass-licker.

example:
Jorge les dio regalos de navidad a todos los ejecutivos. No sabía que era un **lameculos**.

translation:
Jorge gave all of the executives Christmas presents. I didn't know he was such a **brown-noser**..

lamehuevos *m.* brown-noser • (lit.): egg (testicles) sucker.

example:
¡Ese **lamehuevos** acaba de ser ascendido!

translation:
That **brown-noser** just got a promotion!

lamepollas *m.* cocksucker • (lit.): [same].

example:
El primo de Pablo es un **lamepollas**. ¡No lo soporto!

translation:
Pablo's cousin is a **cocksucker**. I can't stand him!

largo al pedo *m. (Argentina)* tall man • (lit.): long or tall fart.

example:
¡Qué **largo al pedo**! Debe ser jugador de baloncesto.

translation:
What a **tall man**! He must be a basketball player.

VARIATION: lungo al pedo *m.*

maldita puta *f.* damned bitch • (lit.): damned whore.

example:
¡Esa **maldita puta** ha derramado jugo de tomate en mi chaleco nuevo!

translation:
That **bitch** spilled tomato juice on my new sweater!

mamón/ona *n. & adj.* • **1.** brown-noser • **2.** obnoxious person.

example:
Rolando le ha comprado el almuerzo al jefe por tercera vez en esta semana. ¡Qué **mamón**!

translation:
Rolando bought the boss lunch for the third time this week. What a **brown-noser**!

NOTE: This is from the verb *mamar* meaning "to suck."

¡Me cago en tu madre! *exp.* Fuck you! • (lit.): I shit on your mother!

example:
¡Cómo eres capaz de hacerme
eso! ¡**Me cago en tu
madre**!

translation:
How dare you do such a mean
thing to me! **Fuck you**!

VARIATION: ¡**Me cago en el
recontracoño de tu
reputísima madre!** *exp.*
(*Cuba – extremely vulgar*)
• (lit.): I shit on the super cunt
of your super whore mother!

**molesto/a como mosca de
letrina** *exp.* annoying
• (lit.): annoying as an
outhouse fly.

example:
¡Vete! ¡Eres **molesto como
una mosca de letrina**!

translation:
Go away! You're **so
annoying**!

papayón/ona *n. & adj. (Cuba)*
asshole, jerk; jerky • (lit.): big
vagina (since *papaya* is used to
mean "vagina" in Cuba).

example:
¿Has invitado tú a esa
papayón a la fiesta?

translation:
You invited that **asshole** to
your party?

pedazo de pelotudo *m.*
(*Argentina*) jerk, idiot
• (lit.): piece of someone
with balls.

example:
¡Le dejé mi coche a Jaime y
el **pedazo de pelotudo**
lo estrelló contra una pared!

translation:
I lent my car to Jaime and
that **idiot** crashed it into a
wall!

pelotas *n. & adj. (Colombia)*
dumbbell, idiot; stupid
• (lit.): that which has with
balls.

example:
¡Antonio se lavó el pelo con
pasta dentrífica! ¡Qué
pelotas!

translation:
Antonio accidentally
washed his hair with
toothpaste! What an **idiot**!

pelotudo y boludo *exp.*
(*Argentina*) said of someone
who is an extreme asshole
with a great deal of nerve
(or "balls") • (lit.): balled
and balled.

example:
¡Armando ha intentado
ligarse a mi novia!
¡Verdaderamente es un
pelotudo y un boludo!

translation:
Armando just tried to pick up my girlfriend! He **really has nerve**!

pendejo/a *n. & adj. (Mexico)* fucker; fucked (said of a contemptible person).

example:
¡Ese **pendejo** acaba de tirar un huevo en mi carro!

translation:
That **fucker** just threw an egg at my car!

pesado/a *n. & adj.* pain-in-the-neck; annoying
• (lit.): heavy.

example:
Ahí está Monica. No quiero que me vea; ¡es tan **pesada**!

translation:
There's Monica. I don't want her to see me. She's so **annoying**!

pinche *n. & adj.* tightwad; stingy, cheap • (lit.): scullion, kitchen boy.

example:
Diego es un **pinche**. ¡No me invitó ni a un café el día de mi cumpleaños!

translation:
Diego is so **cheap**. He didn't even offer to buy me a cup of coffee for my birthday!

plomo/a *n. (Argentina)* annoying (said of a person)
• (lit.): lead.

example:
Un amigo mío se queda en mi casa una semana más. Al principio no me molestaba, pero se está convirtiendo en un **plomo**.

translation:
A friend of mine is staying at my house for another week. I didn't mind at first, but he becoming more and more a **pain-in-the-ass**!

puta madre *f. (Mexico)* mother fucker • (lit.): mother.

example:
¡Esa **puta madre** me acaba de dar una patada!

translation:
That **mother fucker** just kicked me!

NOTE: In Spanish, to talk about someone's mother disparagingly is a prelude to a fight.

ALSO: **me vale madre** *exp.* I don't give a fuck • (lit.): it's worth a mother to me.

puto *m. & adj.* derogatory for "homosexual," fag; faggy.
• (lit.): male/female prostitute.

example:
Benito es un **puto** de gustar los hombres altos.

translation:
Benito is a **fag**. He likes tall men.

NOTE: **puta** *f. & adj.* prostitute, slut.

putonero/a *n. & adj.* from the feminine noun *puta* meaning "whore" • (lit.): one who likes whores.

example:
Ese tío es un **putonero**, siempre anda con mujerzuelas.

translation:
That guy's a real **whore-hound**. He is always hanging out with easy women.

¡Sola vaya! *interj. (Cuba)* Good riddance! • (lit.): Just go!

example:
¡No vuelvas aquí nunca! **¡Sola vaya**!

translation:
Don't ever come back here again! **Good riddance**!

soplapollas *m. (Spain)* jackass, jerk • (lit.): cocksucker.

example:
¿Vas a salir con Pablo? ¡Es un **soplapollas**!

translation:
You're going out with Pablo? He's such a **jerk**!

timbón/ona *n. & adj.*
(Mexico) fatso; extremely fat.

example:
Qué vestido tan bonito, aunque estoy **timbona** para ponérmelo.

translation:
What a beautiful dress. But I'm **too fat** to fit into it.

¡Tu puta madre! *interj.*
• (lit.): Your whore of a mother!

¡Vete a hacer puñetas!
exp. (Spain) Fuck off!
• (lit.): Go beat off!

¡Vete a la mierda! *interj.*
Go to hell! • (lit.): Go to shit!

¡Vete al carajo! *interj.* Go to hell! • (lit.): Go to the asshole's house!

¡Vete al coño de tu madre! *interj. (Cuba)* Fuck you! • (lit.): Go to your mother's cunt!

¡Vete al diablo! *interj.* Go to hell! • (lit.): Go to the devil!

vieja conchuda *f. (Argentina)* old woman • (lit.): old cunted one (from the feminine noun *concha*, literally "sea shell," used to mean "vagina" or "pussy").

example:
Nuestra profesora de matemáticas es una **vieja conchuda** que lleva enseñando miles de años.

translation:
Our math teacher is an **old relic** who's been teaching for a thousand years.

vieja tetuda *f. (Argentina)* old woman • (lit.): old one with tits.

example:
Espero que esa **vieja tetuda** no sea la nueva jefa.

translation:
I hope that **old lady** isn't our new boss.

viejo boludo *m. (Argentina)* old codger • (lit.): old one with balls.

example:
Mi médico es un **viejo boludo**, pero es buenísimo.

translation:
My doctor is an **old codger** but he's brilliant.

viejo pelotudo *m. (Argentina)* old codger • (lit.): old one with balls.

example:
¡No me puedo creer que dejen a un **viejo pelotudo** como ese detrás del volante!

translation:
I can't believe that they let an **old codger** like that behind the wheel!

zapato *m. (Argentina)* idiot, jerk • (lit.): shoe.

example:
¿Has visto el sombrero que lleva Miguel? ¡Parece un **zapato**!

translation:
Did you see the hat Miguel is wearing? It makes him look like a **jerk**!

zorra *f.* bitch • (lit.): fox.

example:
¿Has conocido ya a la nueva jefa? ¡Es una **zorra**!

translation:
Did you meet the new boss? She's such a **bitch**!

¿Ya probaste la comida? ¡Yo creía que iba a *vomitar las tripas!*

(trans.): Did you taste the food? I thought
I was going **to vomit**!

(lit.): Did you taste the food? I thought
I was going **to barf my guts up**!

Lección Cuatro · Dialogue in Slang

Isabel: ¡Nancy! Muchas gracias por invitarnos. ¡Lo estamos pasando muy bien!
(*en voz baja...*)
Estoy muriéndome de aburrimiento en esta **pocilga**.

Alfonso: Y el marido de Nancy es un verdadero **cabrón**. Yo creo que no se lo está pasando muy bien.

Isabel: El siempre ha sido un verdadero **aguafiestas**.

Alfonso: ¿Ya probaste la comida? ¡Está **asquerosa**! ¡Yo creía que iba a **vomitar las tripas**!

Isabel: Y su casa es tan **mugrosa**. ¡Oh, no! ¡Mira quien acaba de entrar! Graciela López...¡qué **latosa**! **Habla hasta por los codos**. Es una **cotorra** y una **comadrera**. Me sorprende que la invitaron.

Alfonso: ¡Oye! Ese señor que está a su lado, ¿no es su esposo? Parece un **bombo**.

Isabel: ¡Ya sé! Se ha puesto tan gordo. También creo que se ha vuelto un poco **locote**.

Alfonso: El ha cambiado tanto. La última vez que le vi no estaba tan **pelón**. La verdad es que a él no le han **pasado los años en balde**.

Isabel: Me pregunto si todavía es tan **mujeriego** como antes. Es una verdadera **sabandija**.

Did you taste the food? I thought I was going to vomit!

Isabel: Nancy! Thank you so much for inviting us. We're having such a wonderful time!
(then in a low voice...)
I'm dying of boredom in this **dive**.

Alfonso: And Nancy's husband is such a **jerk**. I don't think he's having a good time.

Isabel: He's always been a real **killjoy**.

Alfonso: And did you taste the food? It's **gross**! I thought I was going to **barf my guts up**!

Isabel: And their house is so **filthy**. Oh, no! Look who just walked in! Graciela Lopez...what a **pain-in-the-butt** she is! **She talks nonstop**. She's a **blabbermouth** and a **gossip**. I'm surprised she was invited.

Alfonso: Hey! Isn't that her husband next to her? He looks like a **fat slob**.

Isabel: I know! He's really put on weight. I also think he's gotten a little **nuts**.

Alfonso: He's changed so much. The last time I saw him he wasn't such a **baldy**. To tell you the truth, he sure **isn't aging well**.

Isabel: I wonder if he's still a **dirty old man** like he used to be. He's such a **creep**.

Vocabulary

aguafiestas *m.* killjoy • (lit.): "water party," one who throws water on a party (thereby dampening the festivities).

example:
Nunca invites a Armando a una fiesta porque es un **aguafiestas**.

translation:
Don't you ever invite Armando to a party because he's a real **killjoy**.

asqueroso/a *adj.* gross • (lit.): disgusting, filthy.

example:
No quiero comer en ese restaurante porque está verdaderamente **asqueroso**.

translation:
I don't want to eat in that restaurant because it's really **gross**.

bombo *adj.* fat person, fatso • (lit.): bass drum.

example:
El novio de Marta es un verdadero **bombo**.

translation:
Marta's boyfriend is a real **fatso**.

> **ALSO -1:** **dar bombo a** *exp.* • (lit.): to make a big deal about something • (lit.): to give a bass drum.

> **ALSO -2:** **de bombo y platillos** *exp.* bombastic, showy • (lit.): of bass drum and cymbals.

> **SYNONYM:** **puerco** *m.* • (lit.): pig.

cabrón/ona *n. (Mexico)* jerk, asshole; jerky • (lit.): big goat.

example:
No quiero ir a casa de Miguel porque es un verdadero **cabrón**.

translation:
I don't want to go to Miguel's house because he's a real **jerk**.

NOTE: In Spain and Cuba, the term *coñazo* is used in place of *cabrón*.

comadrero/a *n.* gossip (as in person who gossips) • (lit.): gossip, gossipmonger.

example:
Siempre que me siento a comer con Rita, me cuenta una historia nueva. Es una **comadrera**.

translation:
Every time I sit down to eat with Rita, she tells me a new story. She's a **gossip**.

NOTE: This term comes from the feminine noun *comadre* meaning "midwife."

cotorra *f.* blabbermouth • (lit.): cockatoo.

example:
Anabel es una **cotorra**. Siempre tiene algo que contar.

translation:
Anabel is a **blabbermouth**. She always has something to say.

NOTE: This term is so popular among Spanish-speakers that it is often used as the verb *cotorrear* meaning "to babble" or "to chatter."

estar un poco locote *exp.* to be a little nuts • (lit.): to be a little crazy.

example:
David está **un poco locote**. Siempre hace cosas raras.

translation:
David is **a little nuts**. He's always doing weird stuff.

SYNONYM -1: **estar mal de la azotea** • (lit.): to be bad in the roof.

SYNONYM -2: **estar un poco ido/a** • (lit.): to be a little gone.

SYNONYM -3: **faltar un tornillo** • (lit.): to be missing a screw.

hablar hasta por los codos *exp.* to talk nonstop. • (lit.): to talk even through the elbows.

example:
No me gusta salir con Eva porque **habla hasta por los codos**.

translation:
I don't like to go out with Eva because she **talks nonstop**.

SYNONYM: **hablar como una cotorra** • (lit.): to speak like a cockatoo.

latoso/a *n. & adj.* annoying person or thing; annoying • (lit.): made of tin.

example:
Sergio es un **latoso**. Siempre está contando chismes.

translation:
Sergio is a **pain-in-the-butt**. He's always gossiping.

VARIATION: **lata** *f.* • (lit.): tin can.

SYNONYM: **fregón/ona** *n. & adj.*

morirse de aburrimiento *exp.* to die of boredom • (lit.): to die of boredom.

example:
Esta noche no tengo nada que hacer. **Me muero de aburrimiento**.

translation:
I have absolutely nothing to do tonight. **I'm dying of boredom**.

mugroso/a *adj.* filthy • (lit.): filthy, dirty, greasy.

example:
Antonio siempre está **mugroso**. Parece que nunca se baña.

translation:
Antonio is always **filthy**. It seems like he never takes a bath.

NOTE: This adjective comes from the Spanish noun *mugre* meaning "dirt."

VARIATION: **mugriento** *adj.*

mujeriego *m. & adj.* playboy, womanizer; womanizing • (lit.): one who chases women.

example:
Alfredo es un **mujeriego**. Cada semana tiene una novia nueva.

translation:
Alfredo is a real **playboy**. He's got a new girlfriend every week.

pasar los años en balde *exp.* not to age well • (lit.): to pass the years in vain.

example:
A Darío **no le pasan los años en balde**. ¡Parece que se ha puesto una máscara para asustar!

translation:
Darío **doesn't age well**. He looks like he's wearing a scary mask!

NOTE: This expression is also used to mean "to waste time." For example: *David pasa los años en balde sin hacer dinero;* David wastes time not making money.

pelón/ona *n. & adj.* baldy; bald • (lit.): large hair.

example:
Un día de estos, Tomás se va ha convertir en un **pelón**, porque su papá perdió todo su pelo cuando tenía solo dieciséis años.

translation:
Someday soon, Tomás is going to be a **baldy** because his father lost all of his hair when he was only sixteen years old.

> **NOTE:** **tener la cabeza como una bola de billar** *exp.* • (lit.): to have one's head like a billiard ball.

pocilga *f.* dive, filthy place. • (lit.): pigpen.

example:
Este hotel es una verdadera **pocilga**. Vámonos a otro lugar.

translation:
This hotel is a real **dive**. Let's go somewhere else.

sabandija *f.* creep • (lit.): bug, insect, vermin.

example:
El marido de Isabel es una verdadera **sabandija**. Yo creo que él no la aprecia a ella.

translation:
Isabel's husband is a real **creep**. I don't think he appreciates her.

> **SYNONYM:** **piojo** *m.* • (lit.): louse.
>
> > **NOTE: -1:** **piojoso** *adj.* lousy.
> >
> > **NOTE: -2:** **piojo pegadizo** *m.* pest, leech (someone difficult to get rid of) • (lit.): sticky louse.

vomitar las tripas *exp.* to barf one's guts up • (lit.): to vomit one's guts.

example:
Cuando vi el accidente de tráfico, me entraron ganas de **vomitar las tripas**.

translation:
When I saw the traffic accident, I felt like **barfing my guts up**.

> **ALSO:** **vomitar/devolver hasta la primera papilla** • (lit.): to vomit even the first soft food (one ever ate).

A CLOSER LOOK:
Sexual Body Parts in Slang

When it comes to inventing colorful slang terms, there is certainly no lack of imagination in the Spanish language as demonstrated by the following list. This list will present you with an array of words and phrases for everything from the top of your head to the bottoms of your feet, with several stops along the way!

Anus

ano *m.* • (lit.): anus.

chicloso *m.* anus • (lit.): made of chewing-gum.

chiquito *m.* a tiny anus • (lit.): very small, tiny.

el de atras *exp. (Mexico)* asshole • (lit.): the thing from the bottom.

estafiate *m. (El Savador)* asshole.

fundillo *m.* anus, asshole.
> **NOTE:** This is a variation of the masculine noun *fondillos* meaning "seat of trousers."

maricón *m.* **1.** anus • **2.** homosexual, "fag" • (lit.): sissy, homosexual, queer.

ojal *m.* • (lit.): buttonhole, slit.

ojete *m.* anal sphincter • (lit.): eyelet, eyehole.
> **NOTE:** In Mexico, this term is also used to describe someone who is a pain-in-the-neck. For example: *Miguel es un ojete;* Miguel is a pain-in-the-neck.

ojo del culo *m.* anal sphincter • (lit.): eye of the ass.

remolino del pellejo *exp. (Mexico)* anus • (lit.): the whirlpool of the skin.

rul *m. (Mexico)* anus.

rulacho *m. (Mexico)* anus.

sunfiate *m. (El Salvador)* anus.

trasero *m.* anus • (lit.): rear.

trastero *m. (Mexico)* anus or asshole • (lit.): storeroom.

Breasts

agarraderas *f.pl. (Mexico)* breasts, "tits" • (lit.): grabbers (from the verb *agarrar* meaning "to take" or "to grab").

alimentos *m.pl. (Mexico)* "tits" • (lit.): **1.** food allowance • **2.** alimony.

calcetines con canicas *m.pl.* sagging breasts • (lit.): socks with marbles.

cántaros *m.pl.* breasts • (lit.): pitcher, wine measure.

chichis *m.pl.* breasts, "tits."

chichona *f.* a woman with big breasts • (lit.): easy, presenting no difficulty.

colgados *m.pl. (Mexico)* sagging breasts of an old woman • (lit.): hanging things (from the verb *colgar* meaning "to hang").

delantera *f.* breasts • (lit.): front part.

limones *m.pl.* breasts • (lit.): lemons.

manchas *f.pl.* breasts, "tits" • (lit.): spots or stains.

margaritas *f.pl.* breasts, "tits" • (lit.): pearls.

melocotones *m.pl.* breasts, "tits" • (lit.): peaches.

melones *m.pl.* breasts, "tits" • (lit.): melons.

pechonalidad *m.* breasts, "tits."

NOTE: This is a variation of the feminine noun *personalidad* meaning "personality."

pechos *m.pl.* breasts, "tits" • (lit.): breasts.

pezon *m.* nipple • (lit.): [same].

pitones *m.pl.* breasts, "tits" • (lit.): budding horns (of a bull, deer, goat, etc.).

repisas *f.pl. (Mexico)* breasts, "tits" • (lit.): shelves.

tener los mangos bajitos *exp. (Cuba)* to have sagging breasts • (lit.): to have low-hanging mangos.

teresas *f.pl.* breasts, "tits" • (lit.): Theresas.

tetas *f.pl.* breasts, "tits" • (lit.): [same].

tetona *f.* woman with large breasts (from the feminine plural noun *tetas* meaning "breasts").

tetorras *m.pl.* breasts, "tits" • (lit.): large breasts, large tits (from the feminine plural noun *tetas* meaning "breasts").

Buttocks

asentaderas *f.pl.* seat, buttocks • (lit.): from the verb *asentar* meaning "to seat."

bufete *m.* buttocks, ass • (lit.): **1.** writing desk • **2.** lawyer's office.

cachas *f.pl.* buttocks • (lit.): cheeks (of face).

cachetes *m.pl.* buttocks • (lit.): cheeks (of face).

cachetes del culo *m.pl.* buttocks • (lit.): cheeks of the ass.

calabazo *m. (Mexico)* buttocks • (lit.): squash, pumpkin, marrow.

culo *m.* ass.

`ALSO -1:` **culo mal asiento (estar un)** *exp.* to be fidgety • (lit.): to have an ass that won't sit right.

`ALSO -2:` **culón** *m.* one with a big ass.

`ALSO -3:` **ir con el culo a rastras** *exp.* • **1.** to be in a jam • **2.** to be broke • (lit.): to go with the ass dragging.

`ALSO -4:` **ir de culo** *exp.* to go downhill, to deteriorate • (lit.): to go on its ass.

`ALSO -5:` **lamer el culo de alguien** *exp.* to kiss up to someone • (lit.): to lick someone's ass.

fondo de la espalda *m.* buttocks • (lit.): lower back.

magras *f.pl.* buttocks • (lit.): slice of ham, rasher.

nalgas *f.pl.* • **1.** buttocks •
2. vagina • (lit.): buttocks.

nalgón *n.* a person with a big
buttocks • (lit.): someone with
a large buttocks.

orto *m.* (*Argentina, Uruguay*) ass
• (lit.): rise of the sun or a star.

pandero *m.* buttocks
• (lit.): large tambourine.

parte de atrás *m.* buttocks
• (lit.): behind part.

parte posterior *m.* buttocks
• (lit.): posterior part.

pompi(s) *m.[pl.]* (*children's
language*) buttocks.

popa *f.* buttocks • (lit.): stern (in
a ship), poop-deck.

posaderas *f.* buttocks
• (lit.): innkeeper.

tener el famban barretoso
exp. (*Cuba*) to have a huge
butt.

trasero *m.* buttocks
• (lit.): back, rear.

Chest

pecho *m.* chest.

Penis

aparato *m.* (*Mexico*) penis,
"dick" • (lit.): apparatus.

arma *f.* penis, "dick"
• (lit.): weapon.

berenjena *f.* penis, "dick"
• (lit.): eggplant.

biberón *m.* penis, "dick"
• (lit.): baby bottle, feeding
bottle.

bicho *m.* penis, "dick"
• (lit.): bug.

broca *f.* penis, "dick"
• (lit.): the bit of a drill.

butifarra *f.* penis, "dick"
• (lit.): pork sausage.

cacho *m.* (*El Salvador*) penis,
"dick" • (lit.): small piece,
chunk.

camote *m.* penis, "dick"
• (lit.): sweet potato.

canario *m.* penis, "dick"
• (lit.): canary.

caoba *f.* *(Cuba)* penis, "dick"
• (lit.): mahogany tree.

capullo *m.* penis, head of the penis.

carajo *m.* penis, "dick"
• (lit.): penis.
NOTE: This term is commonly used in Mexico as an expletive. For example: *¡Carajo!;* Shit!

carallo *m.* penis, "dick."
NOTE: This is a variation of the masculine noun *carajo* meaning "penis."

chaira *f.* penis, "dick"
• (lit.): cobbler's knife.

chiflo *m.* penis, "dick"
• (lit.): whistle.

chile *m.* *(Mexico)* penis, "dick"
• (lit.): chile, hot pepper.

chilito *m.* *(Mexico, Spain)* an insulting term for a little penis • (lit.): small chile, small hot pepper.

choncha *f.* penis, "dick."

chora *f.* penis, "dick"
• (lit.): female thief.

chorizo *m.* penis, "dick"
• (lit.): pork sausage.

chorrico *m.* penis, "dick"
• (lit.): constant flow or stream.

chufle *f.* penis, "dick."

chuperson *m.* *(Mexico)* penis, "dick."

cipote *m.* penis, "dick"
• (lit.): silly, foolish.

cola *m.* penis, "dick"
• (lit.): tail.

cosita *f.* penis, "dick"
• (lit.): little thing.

curo *m.* *(Cuba)* penis, "dick"
• (lit.): leather strap.

daga *f.* *(Puerto Rico)* penis, "dick" • (lit.): dagger.

diablito *m.* penis, "dick"
• (lit.): little devil.

elbi *m.* *(Puerto Rico)* penis, "dick."

elote *m.* penis, "dick"
• (lit.): corn on the cob.

explorador *m.* penis, "dick"
• (lit.): the explorer.

falo *m.* penis • (lit.): phallus,
penis.

fierro *m. (Mexico)* penis, "dick"
• (lit.): iron.

galleta *f. (Costa Rica)* penis,
"dick" • (lit.): cracker, cookie.

garrote *m.* penis, "dick"
• (lit.): club or stick.

hermano pequeño *m.* penis,
"dick" • (lit.): little brother.

hierro *m. (Puerto Rico)* penis,
"dick" • (lit.): iron.

hueso *m.* penis, "dick"
• (lit.): bone.

inga *f. (Cuba)* penis, "dick"
• (lit.): inga plant.

instrumento *m.* penis, "dick"
• (lit.): instrument.

lechero *m.* penis, "dick."
NOTE: This is from *leche*
literally meaning "milk" but
used in slang to mean
"semen."

leña *f. (Cuba)* penis, "dick"
• (lit.): firewood.

longaniza *f.* penis, "dick"
• (lit.): pork sausage.

macana *f.* penis, "dick"
• (lit.): heavy wooden club.

machaca *f.* penis, "dick"
• (lit.): crusher, pounder.

machete *m.* penis, "dick"
• (lit.): machete.

mandarria *f. (Cuba)* penis,
"dick" • (lit.): sledge
hammer.

manguera *f.* penis, "dick"
• (lit.): water hose.

manolo *m.* penis, "dick."
NOTE: This is a variation of
the name *Manuel*.

mazo *m.* penis, "dick"
• (lit.): mallet.

mecasala *f. (El Salvador)*
penis, "dick."

miembrillo *m. (Mexico)*
penis, "dick" • (lit.): small
member.

minga *f.* penis, "dick"
• (lit.): communal work.

minina *f. (child's language)*
penis, "pee-pee" • (lit.): kitty
cat.

mirasol *m.* penis, "dick"
• (lit.): sunflower.

mitra *f. (Puerto Rico)* penis,
"dick" • (lit.): mitre.

mocongó *m. (Puerto Rico)* penis,
"dick."

mona *f. (El Salvador)* penis,
"dick" • (lit.): female monkey.

morcilla *f.* penis, "dick"
• (lit.): blood sausage.

morronga *f. (Central America)*
penis, "dick" • (lit.): a female
cat.

morrongo *m. (Mexico)* penis,
"dick" • (lit.): male cat.

nabo *m.* penis, "dick"
• (lit.): turnip.

ñema *f. (Santo Domingo)* penis,
"dick."
ALSO: macañema *f.*
cocksucker (from the verb
mascar meaning "to chew").

nene *small child (Puerto Rico)*
penis, "dick" • (lit.): small
child.

pacaya *f. (El Salvador)* penis,
"dick" • (lit.): elongated
vegetable.

pajarito *m.* penis, "dick"
• (lit.): small bird.

palo *m.* penis, "dick"
• (lit.): pole, stick.
NOTE: echar un palo
exp. to fornicate • (lit.): to
throw the stick or "penis."

partes *f.pl.* genitals
• (lit.): parts.

partes nobles *f.pl.* penis,
"dick" • (lit.): noble parts.

pedazo *m. (Uruguay)* penis,
"dick" • (lit.): piece.

pelona *f.* penis, "dick."
NOTE: This is from the
adjective *pelón* meaning
"bald."

pepino *m.* penis, "dick"
• (lit.): cucumber.

pesquesuda *f.* penis, "dick."

picha *(Cuba)* penis, "dick."

NOTE -1: **pichada** *f.* fornication, screwing.

NOTE -2: **pichar** *v.* to fornicate, to screw.

pichicuaca *f. (El Salvador)* penis, "dick."

pichón *m.* penis, "dick"
• (lit.): squab.

pichula *f. (Chile)* penis, "dick."
NOTE: This is from the verb *pichulear* meaning "to deceive."

pico *m. (Chile)* penis, "dick"
• (lit.): beak.
NOTE: In some parts of South America, *y pico* is used to mean "approximately": *Te veo a las siete y pico;* I'll see you around seven o'clock.

pijo/a • **1.** *n.* penis • **2.** *adj.* snobby • *¡Qué mujer más pija!;* What a snobby woman!
• **3.** *n.* stupid person.

pimiento *m.* penis, "dick"
• (lit.): pimento, pepper.

pinco *m. (Puerto Rico)* penis, "dick" • (lit.): penis.

pinga *(Cuba, Puerto Rico)* penis, "dick"
• (lit.): shoulder yoke (used for carrying).

pirulí *m.* penis, "dick."

pistola *f.* penis, "dick"
• (lit.): pistol.

pito *m. (Spain, Uruguay)* penis, "dick" • (lit.): horn, whistle.

pizarrín *m.* penis, "dick"
• (lit.): slate pencil.

plátano *m.* penis, "dick"
• (lit.): banana.

polla *f. (Spain)* penis, "dick"
• (lit.): young hen.

popeta *f. (Puerto Rico)* penis, "dick."

porra *f.* penis, "dick"
• (lit.): club, bludgeon.

prieta *f.* penis, "dick"
• (lit.): the swarthy one.

rabo *m.* penis, "dick"
• (lit.): tail.

reata *f. (Mexico)* penis, "dick"
• (lit.): rope.

retazo macizo m. (Mexico) penis, "dick" • (lit.): stiff piece.

riata f. (Mexico) penis, "dick."

rifle m. (Mexico) penis, "dick" • (lit.): rifle.
NOTE: This term is borrowed from English.

rodillo m. penis, "dick" • (lit.): rolling pin.

salame m. (Argentina) penis, "dick" • (lit.): salami.

salchicha f. penis, "dick" • (lit.): sausage.

tolete m. (Cuba) penis, "dick" • (lit.): club.

tornillo m. penis, "dick" • (lit.): screw.

tranca f. (Cuba, Puerto Rico) penis, "dick" • (lit.): club, thick stick.

trasto m. penis, "dick" • (lit.): old piece of furniture, piece of lumber.

trompa f. penis, "dick" • (lit.): horn.

tronco m. (Puerto Rico) penis, "dick" • (lit.): trunk.

vara f. penis, "dick" • (lit.): stick.

velga f. (Puerto Rico) penis, "dick" (from verga meaning "broomstick").
NOTE: In Puerto Rico, it is common to pronounce the "R" as an "L" when it occurs within a word. Even the country itself is often pronounced Puelto Rico by the natives.

verga f. • **1.** penis • **2.** stupid person ("dick-head") (lit.): broomstick.

víbora f. penis, "dick" • (lit.): viper.

yuca f. (El Salvador) penis, "dick" • (lit.): yucca plant.

zanahoria f. penis, "dick" • (lit.): carrot.

Testicles

aguacates m.pl. (Mexico) testicles • (lit.): little avocados.

albondigas *f.pl.* *(Mexico)*
testicles • (lit.): meatballs.

alforjas *m.pl.* testicles
• (lit.): saddlebags.

ayotes *m.pl.* *(Mexico)* testicles
• (lit.): pumpkins.

bolas *f.pl.* testicles • (lit.): balls.

bolitas *f.pl.* testicles • (lit.): little
balls.

cataplines *m.* testicles.

cojinetes *m.* testicles
• (lit.): small cushions.

cojones *m.pl.* testicles, "balls"
• (lit.): testicles.

> **NOTE:** The term *cojones* may
> also be used as an interjection
> of surprise, anger, or
> annoyance. Examples: *No me
> importa dos cojones;* I don't
> give a shit • (lit.): I don't care
> two balls [testicles] about it.
> *¡Cojones!;* Bullshit!
> *¡Y un cojón!;* Like hell it is!
> *Hace falta tener cojones;* You've
> got to have balls [be brave].
> *Es un tipo sin cojones;* That
> guy's a coward • (lit.): That
> guy doesn't have balls
> [courage].

> **NOTE:** **cojonear** *v.* to act like
> a jerk.

colgajos *m.pl.* testicles
• (lit.): bunch (of fruit such
as grapes, etc.).

colgantes *m.pl.* testicles,
"balls" • (lit.): "danglers."

huevos *m.pl.* testicles
• (lit.): eggs.

> **NOTE -1:** In Bolivia, this
> term means "homosexual,"
> or closer, "faggot."

> **NOTE -2:** **costar un
> huevo** *exp.* to be terribly
> expensive, "to cost one's left
> nut" • (lit.): to cost one
> testicle.

> **NOTE -3:** **huevada** *f.*
> stupidity.

> **NOTE -4:** **huevón** *adj.* a
> description of a lazy or
> stupid person • (lit.): one
> with big *huevos* or "balls."

> **NOTE -5:** **tener huevos**
> *exp.* to be courageous
> • (lit.): to have balls.

obstaculos *m.pl.* *(Mexico)*
testicles • (lit.): obstacles.

partes *f.pl.* genitals
• (lit.): parts.

pelotas *f.pl.* testicles
• (lit.): balls.

NOTE: **tener pelotas** *exp.* to have courage • (lit.): to have balls.

pelotas michinadas *f.pl.* (*Mexico, Central and South America*) blue balls.

sopladores *m.pl.* (*Mexico*) testicles • (lit.): blowers, ventilators.

tanates *m.pl.* (*Mexico*) testicles • (lit.): bundle, parcel.

tompeates *m.pl.* (*Mexico*) testicles.

Vagina

almeja *f.* (*extremely vulgar*) vagina, "cunt" • (lit.): clam.

VARIATION: **almejilla** *f.* • (lit.): small clam.

argolla *f.* vagina, "pussy" • (lit.): ring, hoop, band.

bacalao *m.* (*Mexico*) vagina, "pussy" • (lit.): codfish.

bajar al pozo *exp.* (*Cuba*) to eat pussy • (lit.): to go down to the well.

bigote *m.* vagina, "pussy" • (lit.): mustache.

bizcocho *m.* vagina, "pussy" • (lit.): sweet bread or sponge cake.

bollo *m.* vagina, "pussy" • (lit.): a type of bread.

CAUTION: In western Venezuela, the expression *tremendo bollo* means "nice pussy." However, in other parts of the same country, the expression would simply translate as "big mess" or "fine pickle."

bruquena *f.* vagina, "pussy."

cajeta *f.* (*Argentina*) vagina, "pussy" • (lit.): a type of sweet pudding.

casita de paja *f.* (*Puerto Rico*) vagina, "pussy" • (lit.): small house of straw.

cepillo *m.* vagina, "pussy" • (lit.): brush.

chacón *f.* (*Argentina*) vagina, "pussy" • (lit.): an inversion of the feminine term *concha* meaning "sea shell."

VARIATION: **concho** *m.*

chango *m.* vagina, "pussy"
• (lit.): monkey.

chimba *f. (Colombia)* vagina, "pussy."

NOTE: This is a variation of the masculine noun *chimbo* which is a type of dessert.

chocha *f. (Cuba)* vagina, "pussy"
• (lit.): woodcock (a type of game bird).

chocho *m. (Mexico, Spain)* vagina, "pussy" • (lit.): floppy.

chucha *f.* vagina, "pussy"
• (lit.): bitch dog *(Chile)*.

chumino *m.* vagina, "pussy."

cocho *m. (Mexico, El Salvador)* vagina, "pussy" • (lit.): dirty, filthy.

coña *f.* • **1.** vagina • **2.** joking.

NOTE: This is a variation of the masculine noun *coño* meaning "cunt."

ALSO: ¡No me des la coña! *interj.* Fuck off! Don't bother me!

concha *f. (Central America, Cuba, Uruguay, Argentina)* vagina, "pussy" • (lit.): sea shell.

ALSO: ¡La concha de tu madre! *interj.* an extremely vulgar insult literally meaning "¡Your mother's cunt!"

VARIATION: concho *m.*

conejo *m.* vagina, "cunt"
• (lit.): rabbit.

coño *m.* vagina, "cunt."

NOTE: This term is commonly used in many Spanish-countries (with the exception of Mexico) as an interjection denoting surprise, anger, or annoyance. For example: ¡Coño! ¡No sabía que iba a llover!; Shit! I didn't know it was supposed to rain!

crica *f. (Puerto Rico)* vagina, "pussy" • (lit.): vagina.

cuca *f. (Venezuela, El Salvador)* vagina, "pussy"
• (lit.): clever, smart.

cuevita *f.* vagina, "pussy"
• (lit.): little cave.

dona *f.* vagina, "pussy"
• (lit.): doughnut.

finquita f. (Puerto Rico) vagina, "pussy" • (lit.): small piece of property.

gata f. vagina, "pussy" • (lit.): female cat.

grieta f. vagina, "pussy" • (lit.): crack.

hediondito m. vagina, "pussy" • (lit.): the little smelly one.

higo m. vagina, "pussy" • (lit.): fig (fruit).

hoyo m. (Puerto Rico) vagina, "pussy" • (lit.): hole.

lacho m. (Puerto Rico) vagina, "pussy."

mico/a n. (Central America) vagina, "pussy" • (lit.): car jack.

minino m. (child's language) vagina • (lit.): kitty cat.

muñeco m. (Mexico) vagina, "pussy" • (lit.): doll, puppet.

nalgas f.pl. • **1.** vagina • **2.** buttocks • (lit.): buttocks.

nido m. (Mexico) vagina • (lit.): bird's nest or hiding place.

pan m. (El Salvador) vagina • (lit.): bread.

panocha f. (Mexico) vagina, "pussy" • (lit.): sweetbread.

panuda f. (El Salvador) large vagina.

papaya f. (Cuba, Puerto Rico, Central America) vagina, "pussy."

NOTE: In Cuba, the papaya fruit is called *fruta bomba,* or literally, "bomb fruit" (or "fruit shaped like a bomb").

papayón m. (Puerto Rico) vagina, "pussy."

SEE: papaya, *previous entry.*

parrocha f. vagina, "pussy" • (lit.): small pickled sardine.

pashpa f. (El Salvador) vagina, "pussy".

pepa f. vagina, "pussy" • (lit.): take from the female name "Pepa."

pepita *f.* clitoris • (lit.): nugget.

pipa *f.* clitoris • (lit.): pipe (for smoking tobacco).

pipilla *f.* clitoris.

pipote *m.* *(Southern Spain)* clitoris • (lit.): big sunflower seed.

pitaya *f.* vagina, "pussy" • (lit.): tropical cactus with an edible fruit.

pitón *m.* *(Puerto Rico)* vagina, "pussy" • (lit.): budding horn.

pupusa *f.* *(El Salvador)* vagina, "pussy" • (lit.): a tortilla filled with cheese.

raja *f.* vagina, "pussy" • (lit.): gash.

rajada *f.* vagina, "pussy" • (lit.): gash.

rajita *f.* vagina, "pussy" • (lit.): little slit.

rosco *m.* vagina, "pussy" • (lit.): ring-shaped roll of pastry.

seta *f.* vagina, "pussy" • (lit.): mushroom.

tamale *m.* vagina, "pussy" • (lit.): tamale.

tonto *m.* vagina, "pussy" • (lit.): silly, foolish.

torta *f.* *(El Salvador)* vagina, "pussy" • (lit.): cake, torte.

yoyo *m.* *(Mexico)* vagina, "pussy."

Carlos *se pone caliente* cuando ve a las prostitútas en el centro de la ciudad.

(trans.): Carlos **gets excited** when he sees the prostitutes downtown.

(lit.): Carlos **puts himself hot** when he sees the prostitutes downtown.

Carlos: ¡Qué día más bonito hace! ¿Qué te parece si damos un paseo al centro de la ciudad?

Alma: ¿Al centro? ¿Para qué? El centro está lleno de **mujeres de la vida galante, alcahuetes** y **casas de citas.** No tengo ganas de ver a gente **acostarse** con otros. ¡Yo no sabía que las mujeres de la calle **te ponían caliente!**

Carlos: No, nada más es interesantes verlas. Ya sabes, la última vez que pasé por allí, vi a Marco con dos **pirujas.** Le estaba **dando un muerdo** a una de ellas. ¿No te sorprendería si a él le gusta tener un **menage a trois**?

Alma: Bueno, si lo hace, espero que use **guantes.** Desde luego no quiere contraer el **SIDA.**

Carlos: Bueno me imagino que solo quería que le **mamaron la verga** o que le dieran una **buena cogida.** La simple idea de ir a un **prostíbulo**...yo estaría tan nervioso que no se me **pondría duro.**

Carlos gets excited when he sees the prostitutes downtown

Carlos: It's such a beautiful day! What do you say we take a stroll downtown?

Alma: Downtown? What for? That neighborhood's full of **whores**, **pimps**, and **bordellos**. I'm not in the mood to watch people **getting it on** with each other. I didn't realize that the prostitutes **get you so hot**!

Carlos: No, it's just interesting to see. You know, the last time I passed by there, I saw Marco with two of the **sluts**. He was actually giving a **French kiss** to one of them. Wouldn't it be shocking if he liked **three-ways**?

Alma: Well, if he does, I hope he uses a **rubber**. He certainly doesn't want to catch **AIDS**.

Carlos: I suppose he just wanted a quick **blow job** or a **a good lay**. Just the idea of going to a **whorehouse**...I'd be so nervous I wouldn't even be able to **get it up**.

Vocabulary

acostarse *v.* to go to bed (with someone) • (lit.): to go to bed.

example:
A María le gusta **acostarse** con un hombre diferente cada noche.

translation:
Maria loves **to go to bed with** a different man each night.

alcahuete *m.* pimp • (lit.): pimp.

example:
¡Mira las joyas que lleva ese tipo. ¡Parece un **alcahuete**!

translation:
Look at all the jewelry that guy is wearing. He looks like a **pimp**!

guantes *m.pl.* rubber, condom • (lit.): gloves.

example:
Unos **guantes** no te va a proteger siempre de quedarte embarazada.

translation:
A **rubber** won't always protect you from getting pregnant.

SYNONYM -1: camiseta *f.* • (lit.): t-shirt.
SYNONYM -2: capucha *f.* • (lit.): hood (of a garment).
SYNONYM -3: globo *m.* • (lit.): balloon.

casa de citas *f.* bordello, whorehouse • (lit.): a house used for dates
or appointments.

example:
Dicen que hay una **casa de citas** muy famosa en Texas.

translation:
They say there's a very famous **whorehouse** in Texas.

SYNONYM -1: casa de prostitución • (lit.): prostitution house.
SYNONYM -2: prostíbulo • (lit.): whorehouse.

dar un muerdo *exp.* to French kiss • (lit.): to give a bite.

example:
¡Mira! Hector le está **dando un muerdo** a su secretaria.

translation:
Look! Hector is **giving** his secretary **a French kiss**.

mamar/chupar la verga *exp.* to give [someone] a blow job • (lit.): to suck penis.

example:
A Cecilia le encanta **mamar la verga**. La verdad es que creo que está obsesionada con el sexo.

translation:
Cecilia loves to give **blow jobs**. Frankly, I think she's obsessed with sex.

SYNONYM -1: **dar una buena chupadita** *exp.* • (lit.): to give [someone] a good sucking.

SYNONYM -2: **tocar la trompeta** *exp.* • (lit.): to play the trumpet.

ménages à trois *exp.* three-way ("three people having sex together") • (lit.): house of three [people].

example:
No me puedo creer que a Isabel le gustan los **ménages à trois**.

translation:
I can't believe Isabel likes to do **three ways**.

NOTE: This French expression has been incorporated into the Spanish language and is quite common.

mujer de la vida galante *f.* whore • (lit.): woman of luxurious lifestyle.

example:
Ese barrio está lleno de **mujeres de la vida galante.**

translation:
That neighborhood is full of **whores**.

SYNONYM -1: **mujer de la calle** *f.* • (lit.): woman of the street, "street-walker."

SYNONYM -2: **puta** *f.*

SYNONYM -3: **ramera** *f.*

piruja *f.* slut.

example:
A Carlos le gusta andar con **pirujas**.

translation:
Carlos likes to be with **sluts**.

SYNONYM: **putonga** *f.* • (lit.): large whore.

poner caliente *exp.* to turn someone on • (lit.): to put someone hot.

example:
¡Sara me **pone caliente**!

translation:
Sara **turns me on**!

SYNONYM: **calentar** *v.* • (lit.): to heat up.

poner duro *v.* to get it up • (lit.): to turn hard.

example:
Estoy tan nervioso que no sé si se me va a **poner duro**.

translation:
I'm so nervous that I don't know if I'll be able **to get it up**.

prostíbulo *m.* whorehouse • (lit.): whorehouse.
example:
Ese **prostíbulo** es una verdadera verguenza para este pueblo.

translation:
That **whorehouse** is a real embarrassment for this town.

SYNONYM -1: **casa de citas** *exp.* • (lit.): a house used for dates.

SYNONYM -2: **casa de prostitución** *exp.* • (lit.): prostitution house.

SIDA *m.* AIDS • (lit.): SIDA is a common acronym for "Sindrome Inmunodeficiencia Adquirida."

example:
El **SIDA** es una enfermedad mortal que se contagia a través del uso de drogas intravenosas y del sexo.

translation:
AIDS is a deadly disease spread through intravenous drug use and sex.

una buena cojida *f.* (may be used to describe a man or a woman) a good lay.

example:
Ricardo fue a la casa de citas porque quería que le dieran **una buena cojida**.

translation:
Ricardo went to the whorehouse because he wanted **a good lay**.

SYNONYM: **un buen meneo** *exp.* • (lit.): a good move.

A CLOSER LOOK:
Sexual Slang

The Spanish language contains one of the richest and most innovative collection of slang terms and expressions for anything having to do with sex that I have ever heard. You'll notice that many of the following terms are actually treated with a great deal of humor and extreme imagination!

A good lay

un buen meneo *exp.* a good
lay • (lit.): a good move.

un buen revolcón *m.* a good
lay • (lit.): a good rolling
about.

una buena cogida *f.* a good
lay • (lit.): a good fuck.
NOTE: This expression applies
to both men and women.

una buena tranca *f.* a good
lay • (lit.): a good thick stick.

AIDS

SIDA *m.* Sindrome
Inmunodeficiencia Adquirida.

Bestiality

bestialismo *m.* bestiality.

zoofilia *m.* bestiality.

Blow job

chupar/mamar la pinga
exp. to give a blow job, to
suck dick • (lit.): to suck the
"dick."
NOTE: Any slang synonym
for "penis" can be used
here.
SEE: **penis**, *p. 86.*

dar una mamada *exp.* to
give a blow job • (lit.): to
give a sucking.

mamada *f.* blow job
• (lit.): sucking.

tirarse a mamar *exp.* to
give a blow job • (lit.): to
pull oneself a sucking.

tocar la trompeta *exp.* to
give a blow job • (lit.): to
play the trumpet.

Condom

angel custodio *m.* (*Mexico*)
condom • (lit.): guardian
angel.

angel de la guardia *m.*
(*Mexico*) condom
• (lit.): guardian angel.

calcetín *m.* condom
• (lit.): sock.

capucha *f.* condom
• (lit.): hood (of a garment).

capuchón *m.* condom
• (lit.): hood (of a garment).

el sin mangas *exp. (Mexico)*
condom • (lit.): the one
without sleeves.

forro *m.* condom • (lit.): lining,
covering.

funda *f.* condom • (lit.): lining,
covering.

globo *m.* condom
• (lit.): balloon.

goma *f.* condom • (lit.): rubber.

gomita *f.* condom • (lit.): small
rubber.

gorro *m.* condom • (lit.): cap,
bonnet.

guante *m.* condom
• (lit.): glove.

impermeable *m. (Mexico)*
condom • (lit.): raincoat.

manga *f. (Mexico)* condom
• (lit.): sleeve.

paracaídas *m.* condom
• (lit.): parachute.

paraguas *m.* condom
• (lit.): umbrella.

sombrero de Panama *exp.*
(Mexico) condom
• (lit.): Panama's hat.

tacuche de filiberto *m.*
(Mexico) condom
• (lit.): clothing of the filbert
(since *filiberto* is used to
mean "penis" in slang).

Daisy chain

hacer un cuadro *exp.*
(Cuba) to make a daisy
chain • (lit.): to make a
picture.

Dildo

consolador *m.* dildo
• (lit.): comforter, consoler.

Ejaculate

acabar *v.* *(Argentina)* to ejaculate, to have an orgasm • (lit.): to finish • *¡Estoy por acabar!*; I'm going to ejaculate!

correrse *v.* to ejaculate, to have an orgasm.

NOTE: The intransitive form of this verb *correr* literally means "to run." However, in the reflexive form, it carries a sexual connotation.

expulsar *v.* to ejaculate • (lit.): to expel, eject.

gozar *v.* to ejaculate • (lit.): to enjoy.

irse *v.* to ejaculate • (lit.): to leave, go away.

irse a la gloria *exp.* to ejaculate • (lit.): to go to the glory.

irse de la varilla *exp.* to ejaculate • (lit.): to go from the stick.

lanzar *v.* to ejaculate • (lit.): to throw.

regarse *v.* to ejaculate, to have an orgasm • (lit.): to wet oneself.

venirse *v.* *(Mexico)* to ejaculate • (lit.): to come.

Erection

armado (estar) *adj.* to get an erection • (lit.): to be armed.

empalmado (estar) *adj.* to get an erection • (lit.): to be connected.

empalmarse *v.* to get an erection • (lit.): to connect, to join.

enrucado (estar) *adj.* to get an erection.

pararse *v.* to get an erection • (lit.): to stand up.

ponserse duro *exp.* to get an erection • (lit.): to put oneself hard.

tenerla dura *exp.* to get an erection • (lit.): to have it hard.

tenerla tiesa *exp.* to get an erection • (lit.): to have it stiff.

Finger (to)

manosear *v.* to finger [someone] • (lit.): to touch with one's hands.

meter el dedo *exp.* to finger [someone] • (lit.): to put the finger.

Fornicate

cachar *v.* (Peru) to have sex, to fornicate • (lit.): to break into pieces.

casquete (echar un) *exp.* to have a fuck • (lit.): to throw a helmet.

cepillar *v.* to fornicate • (lit.): to brush.

VARIATION: cepillarse a *v.*

chingar *v.* to fornicate • (lit.): to fuck.

clavar *v.* to fornicate • (lit.): to nail.

coger *v.* to fornicate • (lit.): to get, to catch.

NOTE: This verb leads to many embarrassing moments for natives of Spain who travel to other Spanish-speaking countries. In Spain, the verb *coger* simply means "to catch." It would not be unusual for a Spaniard to travel to Argentina, for example, and ask where he could "catch" the bus by using the phrase: *¿Donde puedo coger el autobús?* translated in Argentina (and many other Spanish-speaking countries) as: "Where can I fuck the bus?"

SEE: *Being Obscene Unintentionally*, *p. 175.*

comer *v.* (Peru, Ecuador, Colombia, Chile, Venezuela) to fornicate • (lit.): to eat.

culear *v.* to fornicate.

NOTE: This comes from the masculine noun *culo* meaning "ass."

dar candela por el culo *exp.* (Cuba) to take it up the ass • (lit.): to give fire from one's ass.

encalomar *v.* to fornicate • (lit.): to become overheated.

enjaretarse a *v.* to fornicate
• (lit.): to do (something) in a rush.

entabicar *v.* to fornicate
• (lit.): to board up, to wall up.

fachar *v. (Venezuela)* to fuck a woman.

follar *v.* • **1.** to fornicate, to fuck • **2.** to fart silently • (lit.): to blow with bellows

foquin *adj. (Puerto Rico)* fucking.

> NOTE: This is a Puerto Rican adaptation of the English adjective "fucking."

hacer un favor *exp.* to fornicate • (lit.): to do a favor.

hocicar *v.* to fornicate • (lit.): to root, nuzzle, grub around in.

ir a desgastar el petate *exp. (Mexico)* to have sex • (lit.): to go wear down the bedding.

ir a desvencigar la cama *exp. (Mexico)* to have sex • (lit.): to go break the bed.

ir a hacer de las aguas *exp. (Mexico)* to have sex • (lit.): to go make some water.

ir a la junta de consiliación *exp. (Mexico)* to have sex • (lit.): to go to a meeting.

ir a la lucha super libre a calzón *exp. (Mexico)* to have sex • (lit.): to go see wrestling wearing nothing but underwear.

ir a percudir el cochón *exp. (Mexico)* to have sex • (lit.): to tarnish the mattress.

ir a rechinar la cama *exp. (Mexico)* to have sex • (lit.): to make the bed squeak.

ir a un entierro *exp. (Mexico)* to have sex • (lit.): to go to a funeral.

joder *v.* • **1.** to fornicate, to fuck • **2.** to bother the fuck out of someone.

joder como desesperados *exp.* to fornicate • (lit.): to fuck like desperate people.

joder como locos *exp.* to fornicate • (lit.): to fuck like crazy people.

joderse vivos *exp.* to fornicate
• (lit.): to fuck alive.

limpiar el sable *exp.* to
fornicate • (lit.): to clean the
saber.

**meterla hasta la
empuñadura** *exp.* to
fornicate • (lit.): to put in up
to the sword hilt.

meterla hasta las cachas
exp. to fornicate • (lit.): to put
it up to the buttocks.

meterla hasta los huevos
exp. to fornicate • (lit.): to put
it up to the balls (testicles).

meterla hasta los puños
exp. to fornicate • (lit.): to put
it up to the fists.

metersela a alguien *exp.* to
fornicate • (lit.): to put it in
someone.

mojar [el churro] *exp.* to
fornicate • (lit.): to wet [the
long fritter].

NOTE: churro *m.* a long,
straight fried pastry.

montar *v.* to fornicate • (lit.): to
climb up (on someone).

palo (echar un) *exp.* to
fornicate • (lit.): to throw a
stick or "penis."

NOTE: palo *m.* penis,
"dick" • (lit.): stick, pole.

pasar por la piedra *exp.* to
fornicate • (lit.): to pass by
the stone.

pasar por las armas *exp.* to
fornicate • (lit.): to pass by
the arms.

pisar a *v.* to fornicate
• (lit.): to step on
(someone).

polvo (echar un) *exp.* to
fornicate • (lit.): to throw a
powder.

revisar los interiores *exp.*
(Mexico) to have sex
• (lit.): to check on one's
insides.

romper *v. (Mexico)* to
deflower a girl • (lit.): to
tear, to break down.

**VARIATION: romper el
tambor** *exp.* • (lit.): to bust
open the screen.

singar *v. (Cuba)* to fornicate
• (lit.): to pole or propel
with an oar.

subir al guayabo *exp.*
(*Mexico*) to have sex • (lit.): to
go up to the jelly.

tirar *v.* (*Peru, Ecuador,
Colombia, Chile, Venezuela*)
to fornicate • (lit.): to throw
away.

tirarse *v.* to fornicate • (lit.): to
throw oneself.

tragar *v.* to fornicate.

tubar *v.* to fornicate • (lit.): to
knock down.

Fornicate doggie-style (to)

a cuatro patas *exp.*
doggie-style • (lit.): on all four
paws.

a lo perro *adv.* doggie-style
• (lit.): in the style of a dog.

**dar por donde amarga el
pepino** *exp.* to fornicate
doggie-style • (lit.): to give
where the cucumber is bitter.

dar por [el] culo *exp.* to
fornicate doggie-style • (lit.): to
give by the ass.

encular *v.* to fornicate
doggie-style, to butt-fuck
• (lit.): to enter the *culo*
meaning "ass."

entrar por detrás *exp.* to
fornicate doggie-style
• (lit.): to enter from the
rear.

**meterla de mira quien
viene** *exp.* (*Cuba*) to
fornicate doggie-style, to
fornicate through the anus
• (lit.): to put it in looking to
see who is coming.

**VARIATION: singar de
mira quien viene** *exp.*

Gang bang

sexo tribal *m.* gang bang
• (lit.): tribal sex.
NOTE: This act is
consensual and therefore
not considered rape as is
violacion en grupo.

violación en grupo *f.* gang
bang • (lit.): group violation.
NOTE: This act is nonconsensual and considered rape
as opposed to *sexo tribal.*

Golden shower

lluvia dorada *f.* golden shower • (lit.): golden rain.

NOTE: This is a sexual act where one partner urinates on the other.

Homosexual
(NOTE: All terms for "homosexual" are derogatory and could loosely be translated as "fag")

afeminado *m.* homosexual • (lit.): an effeminate [man].

amaricado • **1.** *m.* homosexual, "fag" • **2.** *adj.* effeminate.

amaricarse *v.* to become homosexual (from the masculine noun *maricón* meaning "fag").

bijirita *f.* (*Cuba*) "fag," queer.

bufo *m.* homosexual, "fag" • (lit.): clownish, comic.

bujarrón *m.* homosexual, "fag" • (lit.): sodomite.

champe *m.* (*Cuba*) homosexual male, "fag."

NOTE: This is a variation of the masculine noun *champí* meaning "a tiny insect."

chuparosa *f.* homosexual, "fag."

NOTE: This is a variation of the masculine noun *chupaflor* meaning "humming bird."

ciendango *m. Cuba*) homosexual, "fag."

cochón *m.* homosexual, "fag."

comilón *m.* (*Argentina*) homosexual, "fag" • (lit.): big eater (of penis).

cua-cua *m.* (*Puerto Rico*) homosexual, "fag" (from the sound made by a duck).

cuarenta y uno *m.* (*Mexico*) homosexual male, "fag" • (lit.): forty-one.

NOTE: This expression may have originated since some people think that if you are over forty and you are not married, you might be a homosexual.

culastrón *m.* (*Argentina*) homosexual, "fag."

NOTE: This is a variation of the masculine noun *culo* meaning "ass."

culero *m.* homosexual, "fag" (from the masculine noun *culo* meaning "buttocks," or closer, "ass").

cundango *m.* homosexual, "fag."

de la acera de enfrente *exp.* homosexual, "fag" • (lit.): (someone) from the other side of the street.

de la cáscara amarga *exp.* homosexual, "fag" • (lit.): (someone) from the bitter peel (of fruit)

de la otra acera *exp.* homosexual, "fag" • (lit.): (someone) from the other side of the street.

de los otros *m.* homosexual, "fag" • (lit.): one of them.

fresco *m.* homosexual, "fag" • (lit.): fresh.

gay *adj.* • (lit.): homosexual, gay.

invertido *adj.* homosexual, "fag" • (lit.): inverted.

jardinera *f.* homosexual, "fag" • (lit.): female gardener.

joto *m.* *(Mexico)* homosexual, "fag" • (lit.): effeminate.

loca *m.* *(Venezuela)* homosexual, "fag" • (lit.): crazy woman.

mamplora *f.* *(El Salvador)* homosexual, "fag."

marchatrás *m.* *(Argentina)* homosexual, "fag" • (lit.): one who goes backward.

marica *m.* homosexual, "fag" • (lit.): magpie.

maricón *m.* homosexual, "fag" • (lit.): homosexual

maricona *f.* homosexual, "fag" • (lit.): homosexual.

mariposa *f.* *(Mexico)* homosexual, "fag" • (lit.): butterfly.

mariquita *f.* homosexual male, "fag" • (lit.): ladybird.

mesero sin charola *m.*
homosexual male, "fag"
• (lit.): waiter without a tray
(since the hand is in an
effeminate position with the
palm facing upward).

pargo *m. (Cuba)* homosexual,
"fag" • (lit.): red snapper.

pato *m.* homosexual, "fag"
• (lit.): duck.

pirujo *m.* homosexual, "fag"
• (lit.): variation of the
feminine noun *piruja*
meaning "an uninhibited
young woman."

pirul *m.* homosexual, "fag."

plumero *m. (Puerto Rico)*
homosexual, "fag"
• (lit.): feather duster.

puto *m.* homosexual, "fag"
• (lit.): sodomite.

quebracho *m. (Mexico)*
homosexual, "fag"
• (lit.): quebracho bark.

quebrachón *m. (Mexico)*
homosexual, "fag"
• (lit.): large piece of
quebracho bark.

tener una vena *exp.* said to
describe a homosexual
• (lit.): to have one vein.

triángulo *m. (Puerto Rico)*
homosexual, "fag"
• (lit.): triangle.

volteado *m.* homosexual,
"fag" • (lit.): turned around.

yiyi *m. (Puerto Rico)*
homosexual, "fag."

Horny

arrecho *adj. (Peru, Ecuador)*
horny • (lit.): sexually
excited.

calentorro/a *adj.* horny.
NOTE: This is a variation of
the adjective *caliente*
meaning "hot."

caliente *adj.* horny, sexually
hot • (lit.): hot.

salido/a *adj.* horny.
NOTE: This is a variation of
the verb *salir* meaning "to
leave."

ser más puta que las
gallinas *exp. (Cuba)* (said of
a woman) to be as horny as a
toad • (lit.): to be as slutty as
the hens.

Kiss

besar con la lengua *exp.* to
give a French kiss • (lit.): to
kiss with the tongue.

beso *m.* • (lit.): kiss.

beso francés *m.* French kiss
• (lit.): [same].

beso negro *m.* a kiss that is
applied with the tongue up
someone's rectum • (lit.):
black kiss.

morder *v.* to give a French kiss
• (lit.): to bite.

morreo *m.* French kiss.

> **NOTE:** This is a variation of
> the masculine noun *morro*
> meaning "snout."

muerdo *m.* a French kiss, a kiss
with the tongue.

> **NOTE:** This comes from the
> verb *morder* meaning "to bite."

Lesbian
(NOTE: All terms for "lesbian" are
derogatory and could loosely be
translated as "dyke")

bollaca *f.* lesbian.

bollera *f.* lesbian, "dyke"
• (lit.): baker.

cachapera *f. (Puerto Rico)*
lesbian, "dyke."

cachapera *f. (Venezuela)*
lesbian, "dyke."

> **NOTE:** This comes from the
> feminine term *cachapa*
> which is a thin pancake,
> usually served stacked.
> Therefore, a stack of
> *cachapas* conjures up the
> image of several vaginas
> stacked one on top of the
> other.

> **NOTE:** **cachapear** *v.* to
> engage in lesbian sex • *Ellas*
> *se estaban cachapeando;*
> They're having lesbian sex.

macha *f. & adj.* lesbian • (lit.):
the feminine form of *macho*
meaning "very masculine."

machorra *f.* lesbian.

> **NOTE:** This is a variation of
> the masculine noun *macho*
> meaning "manly."

marimacha *f.* lesbian, "dyke."

NOTE: This is a variation of the feminine noun *marica* meaning "sissy" and the adjective *macho* meaning "manly."

tortera *f.* lesbian, "dyke"
- (lit.): tortilla maker.

tortillera *f.* lesbian, "dyke"
- (lit.): one who sells tortillas.

Madame
(pertaining to a bordello)

madama *f.* (Mexico) madame of a brothel.

madre superiora *f.* (Mexico) a madame of a brothel
- (lit.): mother superior.

madrina *f.* (Mexico) a madame of a brothel • (lit.): godmother.

madrota *f.* (Mexico) a madame of a brothel.

NOTE: This is a variation of the feminine noun *madrona* meaning "pampering mother."

mariscala *f.* (Mexico) a madame of a brothel.

Masturbate

acariciarse *v.* to masturbate
- (lit.): to fondle oneself.

botarse la cantúa *exp.* (Cuba) to masturbate
- (lit.): to throw the *cantúa* (a candy made of sweet potato, coconut, sesame, and sugar).

botarse la puñeta *exp.* (Cuba) to masturbate
- (lit.): to throw the cuff.

botarse la yuca *exp.* (Cuba) to masturbate • (lit.): to throw the yucca plant.

botarse una paja *exp.* (Cuba) to masturbate
- (lit.): to toss a straw.

casado con la viuda de los cinco hijos (estar) *exp.* (Cuba) to masturbate
- (lit.): to be married to the widow of the five children.

chaquetear *v.* to masturbate.

VARIATION: hacer una chaqueta *exp.* to make a jacket.

hacer una paja *exp.* to masturbate (someone else) / hacerse una paja *exp.* to masturbate oneself • (lit.): to make a straw.

hacer una cubana *exp.* *(Spain)* (said of a man) to reach orgasm by rubbing the penis between a woman's breasts • (lit.): to do it Cuban-style

hacerse las puñetas *exp.* to masturbate • (lit.): to make oneself cuffs.

hacerse un pajote *exp.* to masturbate • (lit.): to make a large straw.

hacerse un solitario *exp.* to masturbate • (lit.): to do a solitary.

hacerse una bartola *exp.* to masturbate • (lit.): to do a careless act.

hacerse una canuta *exp.* to masturbate • (lit.): to make a tubular container.

hacerse una carlota *exp.* to masturbate • (lit.): to do a Carlota *(a woman's name).*

hacerse una chaqueta *exp. (Mexico)* to masturbate • (lit.): to make a jacket.

hacerse una gallarda *exp.* to masturbate • (lit.): to make a galliard (a type of French dance).

hacerse una magnolia *exp.* to masturbate • (lit.): to make a magnolia.

hacerse una paja *exp.* to masturbate • (lit.): to make a straw.

hacerse una pera *exp.* to masturbate • (lit.): to make a pear.

hacerse una sombrillita *exp.* to masturbate • (lit.): to make a little umbrella.

meneársela *v.* to masturbate, to beat off • (lit.): to shake it for oneself.

paja *f.* masturbation • (lit.): straw •*hacer una paja;* to jerk off.

pajero *m.* a person who masturbates.

pelársela *v.* to masturbate • (lit.): to peel it oneself.

pera (hacerse una/la) *exp.* to masturbate, to beat off
• (lit.): to make oneself a pear.

puñeta (hacer) *exp.* to masturbate, to beat off
• (lit.): to make a cuff.

sacudírsela *v.* to masturbate
• (lit.): to shake it oneself.

sobarse la picha *exp.* (*Costa Rica*) to masturbate • (lit.): to fondle the penis oneself.
VARIATION: **sobársela** *v.*

tocársela *v.* to masturbate
• (lit.): to touch it oneself.

veregallo *m.* (*Mexico*) masturbation.

vergallito *m.* (*Mexico*) masturbation • (lit.): small penis.

Menstruate

bandera roja *f.* menstruation
• (lit.): red flag.

mala semana *f.* menstruation
• (lit.): bad week.

periodo *m.* • (lit.): a woman's period.

purgación *f.* menstruation, period • (lit.): purging.

regla *f.* • (lit.): a woman's period.

tener la mecha puesta *exp.* (*Cuba*) to be menstruating, to be "on the rag"
• (lit.): to have the fire on.

Moist

calado/a *adj.* moist
• (lit.): soaking wet.

empapado/a *adj.* moist
• (lit.): soaking wet.

mojado/a *adj.* moist
• (lit.): wet.

Oral sex

hacer la sopa *exp.* to perform oral sex to a woman
• (lit.): to make a soup.

Pimp

abadesa f. (Mexico) pimp
• (lit.): head of the house.

alcahuete m. pimp • (lit.): wild artichoke.

alcaucil m. pimp • (lit.): wild artichoke.

cafiche m. (Chile) pimp.

caficio m. (Argentina) pimp.

chivo m. pimp • (lit.): goat.

cholo m. (Mexico, Puerto Rico) •
1. pimp • **2.** half-breed, the product of a mixed marriage.

chulo m. pimp • (lit.): **1.** pimp
2. cool- looking, flashy.

cortejo m. (Puerto Rico) pimp
• (lit.): escort.

fundillero m. pimp.

gancho m. pimp • (lit.): hook.

jebo m. (Puerto Rico) pimp.

padrote m. pimp • (lit.): large father.

Pregnant

embarazada f.
• (lit.): pregnant.

preñada f. • (lit.): pregnant.
NOTE: This term is not used in Spain.

quedar de encargo exp.
(Mexico) to make pregnant, to "knock up" • (lit.): made to order.

salir con domingo siete
exp. to get prenant by accident • (lit.): to go out with the 7th of Sunday.

Prostitute

ardilla f. (Puerto Rico)
• (lit.): squirrel.

bruja f. whore • (lit.): witch.

buscona f. prostitute
• (lit.): one who searches (from the verb buscar meaning "to search").

calienta culos f. prostitute
• (lit.): ass warmer.

callejera f. prostitute
- (lit.): pertaining to the street.

chapero m. (Spain) male prostitute.

chica de alterne f. prostitute
- (lit.): alternating girl.

cobo m. (Puerto Rico) old whore
- (lit.): gigantic snail.

congalera f. prostitute, "whore"
- (lit.): someone who works at a bordello.

corbejo m. (Puerto Rico) old whore.

cualquiera f. prostitute
- (lit.): anyone.

cuero m. (Puerto Rico) prostitute who is into leather
- (lit.): leather.

cusca f. prostitute, slut
- (lit.): prostitute.

del rejue exp. (Guatemala, Mexico) prostitute.

del rejuego exp. (Guatemala, Mexico) prostitute.
> **NOTE:** This is a variation of: del rejue.

fulana f. prostitute
- (lit.): so-and-so (anyone).

furcia f. prostitute • (lit.): doll, chick.

garraleta f. cheap whore.

golfa f. prostitute •
(lit.): prostitute.

gorrona f. prostitute
- (lit.): libertine.

guerrillera f. (Puerto Rico) prostitute, whore
- (lit.): guerrilla, partisan.

jaina f. prostitute.

jeba f. (Puerto Rico) prostitute, whore.
> **NOTE:** This is a variation of the masculine noun jebe meaning "alum."

josiadora f. (Puerto Rico) prostitute, whore.

lagarta f. • **1.** prostitute, whore • **2.** bitch
- (lit.): lizard.

maleta f. prostitute, whore
- (lit.): suitcase.

muchachas putierrez *f.pl.*
(*Mexico, Guatemala*) prostitutes
• (lit.): Putierrez girls.

NOTE: The feminine noun
putierrez is a variation of the
term *puta* meaning prostitute
and is used here in jest as the
girls' last name.

mujer de la calle *f.* prostitute
• (lit.): a woman of the street.

mujer de la vida galante *f.*
prostitute • (lit.): woman of
luxurious lifestyle.

mujer fatal *f.* prostitute
• (lit.): wicked woman.

pahuela *f.* prostitute, whore.

pendona *f.* prostitute, whore
• (lit.): despicable person.

pepereche *m.* (*El Salvador*)
prostitute, whore.

perdida *f.* prostitute • (lit.): lost.

pingo *m.* prostitute, whore.

pingona *f.* prostitute, whore.

pluma *f.* prostitute
• (lit.): feather.

puta *f.* prostitute, whore.

ALSO -1: **de puta madre**
exp. • **1.** said of something
excellent • *Esa casa es de
puta madre;* That house is
excellent • **2.** to be in
excellent shape • *Esa tipa
está de puta madre;* That girl
is in great shape.

ALSO -2: **ir de putas** *exp.*
to walk the streets.

ALSO -3: **putada** *f.* annoyance, pain-in-the-neck.

NOTE: The term *puto/a* is
commonly used in place of
the adjectives *jodido/a* and
chingado/a both meaning
"fucking":
*ese jodido/chingado/puto
examen;* that fucking test.

puta de mierda *f.*
(*Argentina*) smelly whore
• (lit.): whore of shit.

putonga *f.* prostitute
• (lit.): large prostitute,
whore.

ramera *f.* prostitute
• (lit.): prostitute, whore.

retozona • **1.** *f.* (*Mexico*)
prostitute • **2.** *adj.* frisky.

rule *m.* (*Mexico*) prostitute.

ruletera *f.* (*Mexico*)
prostitute.

señorita de compañía *f.*
prostitute • (lit.): call-girl.

taconera *f. (Mexico)* prostitute.
NOTE: This comes from the
verb *taconear* meaning "to tap
one's heels."

talonera *f.* prostitute
• (lit.): someone who walks
very quickly.

tana *f. (Mexico)* prostitute.

Red-light district

zonas (las) *f.pl.* red-light
districts in Mexico and
Colombia • (lit.): areas (the).

Semen

crema *f.* semen • (lit.): cream.

jugo *m.* semen • (lit.): juice.

leche *f.* semen • (lit.): milk.
NOTE: This term may also be
used as an expletive.
ALSO -1: **de mala leche** *adj.*
said of someone who is mean
• (lit.): of bad semen.

ALSO -2: **hay mucha
mala leche entre ellos**
exp. there are a lot of bad
feelings between them
• (lit.): there's a lot of bad
semen between them.
ALSO -3: **tener mala
leche** *exp.* to be in a bad
mood • (lit.): to have bad
semen.

licor *m.* semen • (lit.): liquor.

mermelada de membrillo
f. (Mexico) semen
• (lit.): marmalade of the
smaller limb.

néctar *m.* semen
• (lit.): nectar.

Tampon

caballo *m.* tampon
• (lit.): horse.

Threesome

ménage à trois *m.*
threesome • (lit.): house of
three people.

trío *m.* threesome • (lit.): trio.

To look for sex

buscar flete *exp. (Cuba)* to look for some ass • (lit.): to look for freight, cargo.

Whorehouse

aduana *f. (Mexico)* whorehouse • (lit.): Customs.

berreadero *m. (Mexico)* whorehouse • (lit.): a place where one can listen to animals bleat.

casa de citas *f.* whorehouse • (lit.): a house where one can have a date.

casa de putas *f.* whorehouse • (lit.): house of whores.

prostíbulo *m.* whorehouse (from the masculine noun *prostituto* meaning "prostitute").

quilombo *n. (Argentina, Uruguay)* whorehouse.

> **NOTE:** This term is commonly used in Argentina and Uruguay as an interjection: *Qué quilombo!;* What a mess!

resbalón *m. (Mexico, Guatemala)* whorehouse, brothel.

¡Jorge *se echó* un pedo en público!

(trans.): Jorge **farted** in public!

(lit.): Jorge **threw a fart** in public!

Arnoldo: Antes de que nos vayamos tengo que **echar una meada**.

Oscar: ¿Estás seguro? **Apesta a muertos** en esos **cagaderos**. ¡El olor a **mierda** me da ganas de **echar hasta la primera papilla**!

Arnaldo: Por cierto, ¡creo que tu hermanito se acaba de **tirar un pedo** en público o se acaba de **echar un mojón** en sus pantalones!

Oscar: Jorge, ¡otra vez!

Jorge farted in public!

Arnaldo: Before we leave, I need to **take a leak**.

Oscar: Are you sure? It **stinks like crazy** in those **shit-houses**. The smell of **shit** makes me want **to barf up my guts**!

Arnaldo: Speaking of which, I think your little brother either just **farted** in public or **took a dump** in his pants!

Oscar: Jorge, not again!

Vocabulary

apestar a muertos *exp.* to stink like crazy • (lit.): to stink like dead people.

example:
Ese tipo necesita bañarse. **Apesta a muertos**.

translation:
That guy needs to take a bath. **He stinks like crazy**.

cagadero *m.* shithouse • (lit.): a place where one shits.

example:
¡No puedo encontrar el **cagadero** en este tren!

translation:
I can't find the **shithouse** in this train!

echar hasta la primera papilla *exp.* to barf up one's guts • (lit.): to throw up even the first soft food (one ever ate).

example:
Cada vez que me subo a un barco, **echo hasta la primera papilla**.

translation:
Every time I get on a boat, **I barf my guts up**.

echar un mojón *exp.* to take a dump • (lit.): to throw a shit.

example:
Ese perro **echó un mojón** justo en frente de mi casa.

translation:
That dog **took a dump** right in front of my house.

SYNONYM -1: **echar una cagada** *exp.* • (lit.): to throw a shit.

SYNONYM -2: **echar una mierda** *exp.* • (lit.): to throw a shit.

echar una meada *exp.* to take a leak • (lit.): to throw urine.

example:
¡Después de beber tanto café, necesito **echar una meada**!

translation:
After drinking so much coffee, I really need **to take a leak**!

SYNONYM -1: **cambiar el agua al canario** *exp.* (lit.): to change the canary's water.

SYNONYM -2: **echar una firma** *exp.* • (lit.): to make a signature.

echarse/tirarse un pedo *exp.* to let one go, to fart • (lit.): to throw/make a fart.

example:
Aquí huele muy mal. Parece que Carlos se ha **tirado un pedo** otra vez.

translation:
It smells really bad in here. I think Carlos **let one go** again.

VARIATION -1: **tirarse un peillo** *exp.*

VARIATION -2: **tirarse un peo** *exp.*

mierda *f.* shit, piece of shit • (lit.): shit.

example:
Este carro es una **mierda**. ¡Se rompe una vez por semana!

translation:
This car is a piece of **shit**. It breaks down once a week!

A CLOSER LOOK -1:
Bodily Functions & Sounds

Adults often comment about children's preoccupation with "toilet humor" and talking about bodily functions and sounds. Well, kids, move over and make room for your parents, because the following extensive list was created by grown-ups!

Burp (to)

echar un erupto *exp.* to burp
 • (lit.): to throw an eruption.

example:
¡Luis **echó un erupto** en medio de la clase!

translation:
Luis **burped** in the middle of class!

Constipated

andar con mal tapón *exp.*
 (Mexican) to be constipated
 • (lit.): to walk around with a defective cork.

example:
No me encuentro bien. **Ando con mal tapón**.

translation:
I don't feel well. **I'm constipated**.

Defecate (to)

bosta *f.* turd, cow dung
 • (lit.): cow dung.

example:
Cuidado por donde andas. El pasto está lleno de **bosta**.

translation:
Be careful where you walk. The grass is full of **turds**.

cagadero *m.* bathroom, "shithouse" (from the verb *cagar* meaning "to shit").

example:
Antes de salir, tengo que ir al **cagadero**.

translation:
Before we leave, I need to go to the **shithouse**.

cagar *v.* to defecate • (lit.): to shit.

example:
¡Ese niño está **cagando** en la acera!

translation:
That little kid is **shitting** on the sidewalk!

cerote m. (Nicaragua) turd
 • (lit.): large zero.

example:
Algo huele fatal. ¿Has pisado un **cerote**?

translation:
Something smells terrible. Did you step in a **turd**?

churro m. • **1.** turd • **2.** penis, "dick" • (lit.): long fritter (churro; a long, straight fried pastry).

example:
¡Ese perro acaba de echar el mayor **churro**!

translation:
That dog just laid the biggest **turd**!

NOTE -1: The noun churro is also used to refer to a failure. For example: La película fue un churro; The movie was a bomb.

NOTE -2: In Colombia, a churro means "a sexy guy."

desocupar v. to defecate
 • (lit.): to empty.

example:
¡Huele como si alguien hubiera **desocupado** dentro del tren!

translation:
It smells like people **crapped** in this train!

jiñar v. • **1.** to defecate • **2.** to urinate.

example:
Es ilegal **jiñar** en la acera.

translation:
It's illegal **to crap** on the sidewalk.

obrar v. to defecate • (lit.): to perform or to build.

example:
Si tu perro **obra** en la acera, tienes que limpiarlo.

translation:
If your dog **craps** on the sidewalk, you need to clean it up.

quitarle al mondongo un peso de encima exp. (Mexico) to defecate
 • (lit.): to empty out the intestines.

example:
He desayunado tanto que tengo que **quitarle al mondongo un peso de encima**.

translation:
I ate so much breakfast that I think I need **to take a dump**.

regir v. (Mexico) to defecate • (lit.): to rule.

example:
Creo que el niño se ha **regido** otra vez en los pantalones.

translation:
I think the baby **pooped** in his pants again.

zurrar v. to defecate • (lit.): to reprimand, to hit.

example:
Si tienes que **zurrar**, usa el otro baño. Este está roto.

translation:
If you need **to take a dump**, use the other toilet. This one isn't working.

NOTE -1: In Argentina, this verb means "to fart silently."

NOTE -2: zurullo/zurullón m. turd • (lit.): hard lump.

zurullo m. turd • (lit.): hard lump.

example:
Cuidado donde juegas. Hay muchos **zurullos** en este parque.

translation:
Be careful where you play. There are **turds** all over this park.

zurullón m. turd • (lit.): hard lump.

example:
¡Ah, no! ¡He pisado un **zurullón** y he estropeado mis zapatos nuevos!

translation:
Oh, no! I stepped in a **turd** and ruined my new shoes!

Diarrhea

andar con el estómaco flojo exp. (Mexican) to have diarrhea • (lit.): to walk around with a loose stomach.

example:
No puedo ir contigo al cine; **ando con el estómaco flojo**.

translation:
I can't go with you to the movies. **I have diarrhea**.

obraderas f.pl. (Mexico) diarrhea (from the verb *obrar* meaning "to make a bowel movement").

example:
Si bebes agua en ese país, puedes coger **obraderas**.

translation:
If you drink the water in that country, you may get **diarrhea**.

seguidillas *f.pl. (Mexico)*
diarrhea, "the runs"
• (lit.): flamenco song and dance

example:
Me duele el estómago. Creo que voy a tener **seguidillas**.

translation:
My stomach hurts. I think I'm going to have **the runs**.

Fart (to)

bufa *f.* fart • (lit.): jest, piece of buffoonery.

example:
¡Qué peste! Huele a **bufa**.

translation:
What's that odor? It smells like a **fart**.

carapedo *m.* stupid, fart-face
• (lit.): fart-face.

example:
¡**Carapedo**! ¡Déjame en paz!

translation:
Stupid! Leave me alone!

cuesco *m.* fart • (lit.): stone, punch.

example:
¡Acabo de oír al vecino tirarse un **cuesco**!

translation:
I just heard the next door neighbor **fart**!

de pedo *adv.* by luck
• (lit.): by fart (something that happens as easily as a fart).

example:
Gané el concurso **de pedo**.

translation:
I won the contest **by luck**.

discreto/a como pedo de monja *exp.* to be indiscreet
• (lit.): as discrete as a nun's fart.

example:
No me puedo creer que le gritaras a nuestros invitados desde la otra punta de la habitación para decirle que ella tenía un trozo de espinacas al lado de la boca. ¡Fuiste **discreto como pedo de monja**!

translation:
I can't believe that you yelled across the room to our hostess and told her that she had spinach hanging from her mouth. That was **very subtle**!

follar v. • **1.** to fart silently • **2.** to have sex.

example -1:
Algo huele mal. Creo que el niño se ha **follado**.

translation:
Something smells funny. I think the baby **farted**.

example -2:
Verónica es una mujer muy bella. Me encantaría **follármela**.

translation:
Veronica is a beautiful woman. I would love **to have sex with her**.

NOTE: **follón** m. a silent fart, an SBD ("silent but deadly"). See next entry.

VARIATION -1: **follarse** v.

VARIATION -2: **follonarse** v.

follón m. • **1.** silent fart, an SBD ("silent but deadly") • **2.** jam, mess.

example -1:
¡Creo que el niño se ha tirado un **follón**!

translation:
I think the baby let lose an **SBD**!

example -2:
¡Carlos se metió en un **follón**!

translation:
Carlos got himself into a **real jam**!

follonarse v. to fart silently.

example:
Después de comerme toda esa comida picante, creo que voy a **follonarme**.

translation:
After eating all that spicy food, I think I'm going **to fart**.

NOTE: This is a variation of the term **follar**.

mal aire m. fart • (lit.): bad air.

example:
¡Qué asco! ¡Creo que huelo un **mal aire**!

translation:
Yuck! I think I smell a **fart**!

pederse v. to fart • (lit.): to fart.

example:
¡No me puedo creer que **te pedas** en mi coche!

translation:
I can't believe **you'd fart** in my car!

pedo m. • **1.** fart • **2.** drunkenness • **3.** ugly.

example -1:
Ese chiste es tan gracioso
como un **pedo** en un traje
espacial.

translation:
That joke is as funny as a **fart**
in a space suit.

example -2:
Manolo agarró un buen **pedo**
en la fiesta.

translation:
Manolo got really **drunk** at
the party.

example -3:
Ese tipo es un **pedo**.

translation:
That guy is an **ugly person**.

pedorrera f. many farts, a series
 of farts.

example:
¿Has oído esa **pedorrera**?
¡Qué asco!

translation:
Did you hear **all that
farting**? That's disgusting!

pedorrero m. one who farts a
 lot, farter.

example:
Mi tío tiene problemas de
estómago. Es un **pedorrero**.

translation:
My uncle has gastric problems.
He's a **farter**.

peerse v. to fart • (lit.): to fart

example:
Es de mala educación
peerse en público.

translation:
It's rude **to fart** in public.

traque m. loud fart
 • (lit.): loud bang.

example:
¿Has oído ese **traque**?
¡Sonó como si alguien
explotó!

translation:
Did you hear that **loud
fart**? It sounded like
someone exploded!

zullarse v. to fart • (lit.): to
 fart.

example:
La próxima vez que tengas
que **zullarte**, por favor
levántate de la mesa.

translation:
The next time you have **to
fart**, please leave the table.

zullón m. fart • (lit.): fart.

example:
¡Hay un **zullón** que ha
estado pululando por esta
habitación durante una
hora!

translation:
There's a **fart** that's been lingering in this room for an hour!

Shit

cagada *f.* shit (from the verb *cagar* meaning "to shit").

example:
Los fertilizantes están realmente hechos de **cagadas**.

translation:
Fertilizer is actually made of **shit**.

truño *n.* shit.

example:
Ten cuidado de no pisar un **truño**. Hay muchos perros en este barrio.

translation:
Be careful not to walk in any **shit**. There are a lot of dogs in this neighborhood.

Spit (to)

escupir *v.* to spit • (lit.): to spit.

example:
Es ilegal **escupir** en el tren.

translation:
It's illegal **to spit** in the train.

Stink (to)

apestar *v.* to stink • (lit.): to infect with the plague.

example:
Verdaderamente **apesta** aquí. Me pregunto si hay una mofeta cerca.

translation:
It really **stinks** here. I wonder if there's a skunk nearby.

VARIATION: apestar a muertos *exp.* to stink to high heaven • (lit.): to stink to death.

Urinate (to)

cambiarle el agua al canario *exp.* to urinate • (lit.): to change the canary's water.

example:
Antes de salir de viaje, tengo que **cambiarle el agua al canario**.

translation:
Before we leave on our trip, I need **to take a leak**.

chis *m.* (Mexico – *children's language*) urine, piss.

example:
Huele a **chis** en este baño.

translation:
It smells of **urine** in this bathroom.

NOTE: As an interjection, *chis* may be used to mean "shhh!" or "pst!"

cuartito *m.* bathroom, the "john" • (lit.): small room

example:
Necesito ir al **cuartito**.

translation:
I need to visit the **bathroom**.

desbeber *v.* to urinate • (lit.): to "un-drink."

example:
Después de beber toda ese agua, de verdad necesito **desbeber**.

translation:
After drinking all that water, I really need **to take a leak**.

diligencia (hacer una) *exp.* to go to the bathroom (urinate or defecate) • (lit.): to do an errand.

example:
Antes de salir a trabajar, siempre hago una **diligencia** primero.

translation:
Before I leave for work, I always go to the **bathroom** first.

hacer pipí *exp.* to urinate • (lit.): to make pee-pee.

example:
No te olvides de **hacer pipí** antes de irte a la cama.

translation:
Don't forget **to go pee-pee** before you go to bed.

ir a botar el agua al canario *exp.* *(Cuba)* to go take a leak • (lit.): to go to throw away the canary's water.

example:
Creo que he bebido demasiado café; necesito **ir a botar el agua al canario** otra vez.

translation:
I think I drank too much coffee. I need **to take a leak** again.

jiñar *v.* • **1.** to urinate • **2.** to defecate.

example:
¡Tengo que encontrar un sitio donde **jiñar**!

translation:
I need to find somewhere **to relieve myself**!

meadero *m.* urinal (from the verb *mear* meaning "to piss").

example:
El **meadero** en este baño está
tan limpio.

translation:
The **urinal** in this bathroom
is so clean.

meado[s] m.pl. urine, piss (from
the verb *mear* meaning "to
piss").

example:
El olor a **meado** me pone
enfermo.

translation:
The smell of **urine** makes me
sick.

mear v. to urinate, to piss.

example:
Creo que tengo que llevar a mi
hija al baño. Parece que
necesita **mear**.

translation:
I think I need to take my
daughter to the bathroom. She
looks like she need **to take a
leak**.

NOTE: **mearse de risa** exp.
to laugh so hard as to urinate
in one's pants • (lit.): [same].

meón n. baby, "little pisher"
(from the verb *mear* meaning
"to piss").

example:
¿Has visto a ese **meón**?
¡Es tan lindo!

translation:
Did you see that **little
kid**? He's so cute!

pipí m. (child's language)
urine, pee-pee.

example:
¿Has **hecho pipí** antes de
irte a la cama?

translation:
Did you **go pee-pee** before
going to bed?

NOTE: **hacer pipí** exp. to
go pee-pee.

Vomit

un vómito m. (Argentina)
said of anything disgusting
• (lit.): a vomit.

example:
No me voy a comer eso.
¡Parece **un vómito**!

translation:
I'm not eating that food. It
looks **disgusting**!

vomitar hasta la primera papilla *exp.* to vomit, to barf one's guts up • (lit.): to vomit even one's first soft-food.

example:
Estuve tan enfermo la semana pasada, que **vomité hasta la primera papilla**.

translation:
I was so sick last week that **I barfed my guts up**.

vomitar hasta las tripas *exp.* to vomit, to barf one's guts up • (lit.): to vomit up to one's guts.

example:
Creo que anoche me sentó algo mal. Estuve **vomitando hasta las tripas** durante tres horas.

translation:
I think I had food poisoning last night. I was **vomiting my guts up** for three hours.

A CLOSER LOOK -2:
Insults using "Madre" ("mother")

(Note that any attack on one's mother is considered extremely serious and often a prelude to a fight!)

¡Chinga tu madre! *interj.* a common insult meaning "Fuck you!" • (lit.): Fuck your mother!

¡El coño de tu madre! *interj.* (Cuba) Fuck your mother! • (lit.): The cunt of your mother!

¡Hijo de tu chingada madre! *exp.* • (lit.): Son of your fucking mother!

¡La concha de tu madre! *interj.* (Uruguay) an extremely vulgar insult literally meaning "Your mother's cunt!"

VARIATION: **El concho de tu madre!** *interj.*

madre *f.* (Mexico) mother fucker • (lit.): mother.

ALSO: **me vale madre** *exp.* I don't give a fuck • (lit.): it's worth a mother to me.

¡Me cago en la madre que te parió! *exp.* • (lit.): I shit in the mother who gave birth to you!

¡Me cago en tu [puta] madre! *exp.* • (lit.): I shit on your [slut of a] mother!

puta la madre, puta la hija *exp.* like mother, like daughter • (lit.): the mother's a whore, [so] the daughter's a whore.

¡Qué te la mame tu madre! *interj.* • (lit.): May your mother suck it for you!

¡Tu madre tiene un pene! *exp.* • (lit.): Your mother has a dick!

¡Tu madre! *interj.* Your mother!

¡Tu puta madre! *interj.* • (lit.): Your whore of a mother!

¡Vete al coño de tu madre! *interj.* (*Cuba*) Fuck you! • (lit.): Go to your mother's cunt!

LECCIÓN SIETE -The Many Uses of "Mierda"

¿Cómo querrá él que yo coma esa *mierda*?

*(trans.): How does he expect me to eat that **stuff**?*
*(lit.): How does he expect me to eat that **shit**?*

Carmen: Hoy tropecé con Roberta. Me dijo que acaba de heredar un millón de dólares.

Patricia: ¡**Mierda**! ¡Está **llena de mierda**! Te lo juro que ella **tiene la cabeza llena de mierda**.

Carmen: ¡Qué **mierdera**! Ella es una verdadera **mierda**. Se cree que a ella no le **apesta la mierda**. Estuve a punto de decirle que se **fuera a la mierda**.

Patricia: La próxima vez que hable contigo, dile que **coma mierda**. A mí nunca me ha gustado ella.

Carmen: A mí tampoco. ¿Has visto su automóvil nuevo? Es una **mierda**.

Patricia: Ya lo sé. Nunca había visto una **mierdita** como esa en mi vida. Está siempre lleno de basura. Uno de estos días, ¡ella debería de limpiar toda esa **mierda**!

How does he expect me to eat that stuff!

Carmen: Today I bumped into Roberta. She told me that she just inherited a million dollars.

Patricia: ¡**Shit**! She's so **full of shit**! I swear, her **head is full of shit**.

Carmen: What a **scumbag**! She's a real **shit**. She thinks her **shit doesn't stink**. I was so close to telling her to **go to hell**.

Patricia: The next time she talks to you, just tell her to **eat shit**. I've never liked her.

Carmen: Me neither. Did you see her new car? It's **shit**.

Patricia: I know. I've never seen such a **piece of shit** in my life. It's always so full of trash. One of these days, she needs to clean all that **shit** out of it!

Vocabulary

comer mierda *exp.* to eat shit • (lit.): [same].

example:
La próxima vez que me grite mi jefe le voy a decir que **coma mierda**.

translation:
Next time my boss shouts at me I'm going to tell him **to eat shit**.

NOTE: When this expression is transformed into the noun *come-mierda*, the translation becomes "bullshitter."

lleno/a de mierda *exp.* full of shit • (lit.): [same].

example:
Jorge está **lleno de mierda**. Nada de lo que dice es verdad.

translation:
Jorge is **full of shit**. Nothing he says is true.

mierda • **1.** *f.* shit • **2.** *interj.* Shit! • (lit.): shit.

example -1:
Esa tipa es una verdadera **mierda**. Ella nunca es simpática con nadie.

translation:
That girl is a real **shit**. She's never friendly to anyone.

example -2:
¡**Mierda**! ¡Otra vez me dejé las llaves dentro del carro!

translation:
Shit! I locked my keys in the car again!

mierdera *f.* scumbag • (lit.): one who has shit.

example:
Margarita es una **mierdera**. No quiero que venga a mi casa.

translation:
Margarita is a **scumbag**. I don't want her to come to my party.

mierdita *f.* said of somthing defective, piece of shit • (lit.): little shit.

example:
El coche que se acaba de comprar Ana es una **mierdita**. Siempre lo está llevando al mecánico.

translation:
The car that Ana just bought is **a piece of shit**. She's always taking it to the mechanic.

> **SYNONYM:** **porquería** *f.* • (lit.): filth • *Esta casa está llena de porquería*; This house is full of dirt.

pensar/creer que no apesta la mierda de uno *exp.* to be stuck up • (lit.): to think that one's shit doesn't stink.

example:
Lisa es una presumida. **Piensa que su mierda no apesta**.

translation:
Lisa is so stuck up. **She thinks her shit doesn't stink**.

tener la cabeza llena de mierda *exp.* to be stupid • (lit.): to have one's head full of shit.

example:
Rafael **tiene la cabeza llena de mierda**. Nunca se le ocurre una buena idea.

translation:
Rafael **has his head full of shit**. He never has a good idea.

> **SYNONYM:** **tener la cabeza llena de pájaros** *exp.* • (lit.): to have one's head full of birds.

¡Vete a la mierda! *interj.* Go to hell! • (lit.): Go to shit!

example:
¿Cómo me puedes hacer una cosa como esta a mí? **¡Vete a la mierda!**

<u>translation:</u>
How could you do such a thing to me? **Go to hell**!

SYNONYM ·1: ¡**Vete al cuerno!** *interj.* • (lit.): Go to the horn!

SYNONYM ·2: ¡**Vete al diablo!** *interj.* • (lit.): Go to the devil!

SYNONYM ·3: ¡**Vete al quinto coño!** *interj.* • (lit.): Go to the fifth cunt!

A CLOSER LOOK:
The Many Uses of "Mierda"

argolluda/o de mierda n. an insult for a woman • (lit.): big ring of shit (referring to her anus).

barrigón/ona de mierda n. *(Argentina)* said of someone who is very fat • (lit.): potbelly of shit.

bruto/a de mierda n. *(Argentina)* idiot • (lit.): brute of shit.

¡**Ché dejá de dormir, fiaca de mierda, movéte un poco!** *exp. (Argentina)* used in response to seeing a lazy person • (lit.): Hey, stop sleeping, you lazy piece of shit, and move around a little!

coger una mierda *exp.* to get drunk, "shit-faced" • (lit.): to catch a shit.

comemierda n. *(Puerto Rico, Cuba)* jerk • (lit.): shit-eater.

de mierda *adv.* said of something lousy or "shitty," for shit • *Ese regalo que Pedro me dió el día de mi cumpleaños es de mierda;* That gift that Pedro gave me for my birthday was for shit.

Don mierda (ser un) *exp.* to be a real nobody • (lit.): to be a Mr. Shit.

flaco/a de mierda n.
(Argentina) skinny person
• (lit.): thin one of shit.

gordo/a de mierda n.
(Argentina) fat person, fatso
• (lit.): fat one of shit.

lungo de mierda m.
(Argentina) very tall person
• (lit.): long or tall shit.

luz de mierda f. (Argentina)
smart person • (lit.): light of
shit.

mierda (ser una) exp. said of
a despicable person • (lit.): to
be a shit.

mierda • **1.** interj. shit (used to
express surprise, anger,
disappointment) • **2.** filth
• (lit.): shit.

mierdecilla f. • (lit.): little shit.

mierdero m. (Nicaragua) scum
• (lit.): a place where there is a
lot of shit.

mierdita f. a worthless piece of
shit • (lit.): little shit.

mocoso/a de mierda n.
(Argentina) snot-nosed little
brat • (lit.): snotty one of shit.

pendejo/a de mierda m.
(Argentina, Mexico) an insult
in reference to a trouble-
making little child, "piece of
shit" • (lit.): pubic hair of
shit.

**pensar que a uno lo le
apesta la mierda** exp. to
think one's shit doesn't stink
• (lit.): [same].

petiso de mierda m.
(Argentina) short person,
"shrimp" • (lit.): shitty little
one.

puta/o de mierda n.
(Argentina) smelly whore
• (lit.): whore of shit.

una mierda f. (Argentina)
said of something
unpleasant or worthless
• (lit.): a shit.

**¡Vete a la [mismísima]
mierda!** exp. Go to hell!
• (lit.): Go to the [very same]
shit!

**¡Vete a la reverenda
mierda!** interj. (Cuba) Go
to hell! • (lit.): Go to holy
shit!

viejo/a de mierda n. "old
fart" • (lit.): old person of
shit.

¡Y una mierda! exp.
Bullshit! • (lit.): And a shit!

LECCIÓN OCHO - The Many Uses of "Cagar"

Ernesto se estaba *cagando en los pantalones* el primer día en su nueva escuela.

(trans.): Ernesto was **scared shitless** his first day in the new school.

(lit.): Ernesto was **shitting in his pants** his first day in the new school.

Lección Ocho · Dialogue in Slang

Ernesto: Espero que hice bien el examen de biología. ¡**Me cago en los pantalones** porque si no saco una buena nota, mis padres me van a matar. ¡Odio la biología!

Norma: ¡Vaya! También **te cagaste en los pantalones** tu primer día de escuela y todo salió bien después de todo. Créeme. **Tanto pedo para cagar aguado**. La verdad es que yo **me cago de gusto** en la clase de biología. ¡Mira! La maestra está repartiendo los exámenes en este momento.

Ernesto: ¡Qué **cagada**! ¡Me dieron una F! ¡**Me cago en la mar**! ¡La maestra está **cagada**! ¡**Me cago en su puta madre**!

Norma: **No es para cagarte**. Simplemente estudia más la próxima vez.

Ernesto: **Estoy cagado de miedo** si me dan otra F, ¡no voy a poder graduarme de la escuela!

Ernesto was scared shitless his first day in the new school.

Ernesto: I hope I did well on the biology test. **I'm scared shitless** because if I don't get a good grade, my parents are going to kill me. I hate biology!

Norma: Come on! You were also **scared shitless** your first day of school and everything turned out fine. Believe me. **You're getting all worked up about nothing**. Frankly, biology **is a real turn on to me**. Oh, look! The teacher is handing our tests back now.

Ernesto: I'm **up shit creek**! I got an F! **Fuck that shit**! That teacher is **fucked**! **Fuck her**!

Norma: **It's not such a fucking deal**. Just study more next time.

Ernesto: **I'm shit-scared** that if I get another F, I won't be able to graduate from school!

Vocabulary

cagado/a (estar) *exp.* to be fucked • (lit.): to be shit.

example:
Ese arbitro **está cagado**. Está ayudando al equipo local.

translation:
That referee **is fucked**. He's helping the local team.

cagado/a de miedo (estar) *exp.* to be shit-scared • (lit.): to be scared with shit.

example:
Estoy cagado de miedo porque dicen que va a ver otro gran terremoto.

translation:
I'm shit-scared because they say there's going to be another big earthquake.

SYNONYM: **muerto/a de miedo (estar)** *exp.* (lit.): to be dead with fear.

cagarse de gusto *exp.* to be a real turn on to someone, to really like something or someone. • (lit.): to shit with pleasure.

example:
¡**Me cagué de gusto** cuando vi a María en bikini!

translation:
It was a real turn on when I saw Maria wearing a bikini!

SYNONYM: **morirse de gusto** *exp.* • (lit.): to die of pleasure.

cagarse en los pantalones *exp.* to be scared shitless • (lit.): to shit in one's pants.

example:
¡Me **cagué en los pantalones** cuando vi a ese perro grande corriendo hacia mí!

translation:
I was **scared shitless** when I saw that big dog running toward me!

¡Me cago en la mar! *interj.* *(Spain)* Fuck that shit! • (lit.): I shit in the sea!

example:
¡Me **cago en la mar**! ¡Otra vez perdí!

translation:
Fuck that shit! I lost again!

¡Me cago en su puta madre! *interj.* Fuck him! • (lit.): I shit in his whore mother!

example:
Ese tipo me ha robado todo mi dinero. ¡Me **cago en su puta madre**!

translation:
That guy just stole all my money. **Fuck him**!

¡No es para cagarte! *interj.* It's not such a big fucking deal! • (lit.): It isn't to shit!

example:
No es para cagarte. Mañana será otro día.

translation:
It's not such a big fucking deal. Tomorrow's another day.

¡Qué cagada! *interj.* What a fucking mess! • (lit.): What a shit!

example:
¡Qué **cagada**! No tengo ni un centavo a mi nombre.

translation:
I'm up shit creek! I don't have a cent to my name.

tanto pedo para cagar aguado *exp.* to get all worked up about nothing • (lit.): so much farting for such watery shit.

example:
Tanto pedo para cagar aguado. La verdad es que yo creo que te preocupas demasiado.

translation:
You're getting all worked up about nothing. The truth is I think you worry too much.

SYNONYM: **mucho ruido y pocas nueces** *exp.* • (lit.): a lot of noise and very few walnuts.

A CLOSER LOOK:
The Many Uses of "Cagar"

The verb *cagar*, literally meaning "to shit," lends itself to a variety of different shapes; it can be used as a verb, a noun, an adjective, and as the milestone in a number of popular expressions. Even if your journey to a Spanish-speaking country is for a short period of time, you are sure to encounter one of the forms of *cagar* shortly after your arrival, especially if you visit a family with younger members.

cagada *f.* mistake • (lit.): shit.
ALSO: **hacer una cagada a alguien** *exp.* to do something nasty to someone.

cagadero *m.* bathroom, "shithouse."

cagado/a (estar) *adj.* to be full of shit • (lit.): to be shit.

cagada (una) *f.* (*Argentina*) said of something unpleasant • (lit.): a shit.

cagado/a de miedo (estar) *exp.* to be scared shitless • (lit.): to be shit with fear.

cagar *v.* to make a mistake • (lit.): to shit.

cagarse de gusto *exp.* to enjoy something very much
• (lit.): to shit oneself with pleasure.

cagarse en alguien o algo *exp.* to curse someone or something • (lit.): to shit on someone or something.

cagarse en los pantalones *exp.* to be scared shitless
• (lit.): to shit in one's pants (due to fear).

cagarse por las patas abajo *exp.* to be scared to death
• (lit.): to shit in one's pants.

cagitis (tener) *exp.* to have diarrhea • (lit.): to have the shits.

cagón/ona *n. & adj.* coward, scared • (lit.): one who is scared shitless.

culicagado *m.* little kid
• (lit.): shit-covered ass.

¡Esto es cagarse! *exp.* This is a fine mess! • (lit.): This is to shit oneself!

¡Esto es una cagada! *exp.* This is a fine mess! • (lit.): This is a shit!

¡Me cago en la madre que te parió! *exp.* • (lit.): I shit in the mother who gave you birth!

¡Me cago en la mar! *exp.* (*Spain*) Fuck that shit!
• (lit.): I shit in the ocean!

¡Me cago en la purimísima hostia! *exp.* Fuck it all! • (lit.): I shit on the holiest communion wafer!

¡Me cago en tí! *exp.* Fuck you! • (lit.): I shit on you!

¡Me cago en tu puta madre! *exp.* Fuck you!
• (lit.): I shit on your slut of a mother!

¡Me cago en tus huesos! *exp.* • (lit.): I shit in your bones!

¡Me cago en tus mulas! *exp.* • (lit.): I shit in your mules!

¡Qué cagada! *interj.* (*Argentina*) Darn! What bad luck! • (lit.): What shit!

tanta pedo para cagar aguado *exp.* much ado about nothing • (lit.): so much farting for such watery shit.

¡Qué *coño*! ¿Has visto lo que acaba de hacer?

*(trans.): What a **jerk**! Did you see what he just did?*
*(lit.): What a **cunt**! Did you see what he just did?*

Verónica:	¿**Qué coño es esto**? ¡Mira este cuadro! ¡Solo un verdadero **coñazo** hubiera hecho una cosa como ésta! ¡El guardia de seguridad debe de haber estado durmiendo en el trabajo otra vez!
Carolina:	¡**El coño de su hermana**! ¡Ese tipo está siempre durmiendo!
Verónica:	¿**Adónde coño vas**?
Carolina:	Voy a decirle que está despedido.
Verónica:	¡**Siéntate, coño**! A lo mejor no fue su culpa. Al menos dale una oportunidad para que te dé una explicación.
Carolina:	No hay nada que explicar. ¡El tiene que encontrar otro trabajo!
Verónica:	¡**Escúchame, coño**! Tienes que calmarte antes de hablar con él.

What a jerk! Did you see what he just did?

Verónica: **What the hell is this**? Look at this painting! Only a real **asshole** would do something like this! The security guard must have been sleeping on the job again!

Carolina: **Fuck him**! That guy is always sleeping!

Verónica: **Where the hell are you going**?

Carolina: I'm going to tell him he's fired.

Verónica: **For God's sake, sit down**! It may not have been his fault. At least give him a chance to explain.

Carolina: There's nothing to explain. He needs to find another job!

Verónica: **For God's sake, listen to me**! You need to calm down before you speak to him.

Vocabulary

NOTE: In Mexico, the term *coño* is not used. Therefore, in the following examples, a Mexican synonym will always be offered.

¿Adónde coño vas? *exp.* Where the hell are you going? • (lit.): Where the cunt are you going?

example:
¿Adónde coño vas? ¿Es que no ves que está lloviendo?

translation:
Where the hell are you going? Don't you see it's raining outside?

SYNONYM: **¿Adónde carajo(s) vas?** *exp. (Mexico).*

coñazo *m.* **1.** asshole, jerk, pain-in-the-neck **2.** something boring • (lit.): large cunt.

example -1:
Manolo es un **coñazo**. Espero no verle hoy.

translation:
Manolo is an **asshole**. I hope I don't have to see him today.

example -2:
¡Esta película es un verdadero **coñazo**!

translation:
This film is a real **bore**!

SYNONYM: **pendejo/a** *n. (Mexico).*

¡El coño de su hermana! *interj*. Fuck him! • (lit.): His sister's cunt!

example:
¡Paolo me mintió otra vez! **¡El coño de su hermana**!

translation:
Paolo lied to me again! **Fuck him**!

SYNONYM: **¡Hijo de su puta madre!** *interj*. *(Mexico)* • (lit.): Son of your whore mother!

NOTE: It's interesting to note that in Mexico, expressions using *madre* ("mother") are generally negative (as seen in lesson six), whereas expressions using *padre* ("father") are postive! For example: *¡Qué padre!*; That's fantastic!

¡Escúchame, coño! *interj*. For God's sake, listen to me! • (lit.): Listen to me, cunt!

example:
¡Escúchame, coño! No puedes resolver tus problemas por medio de la violencia. Debes de hablar del problema de una manera razonable.

translation:
For God's sake, listen to me! You can't solve your problems through violence. You need to discuss the problem rationally.

SYNONYM: **Escúchame, buey/guey!** *interj*. *(Mexico)*.

¿Qué coño es esto? *interj*. What the hell is this? • (lit.): What the cunt is this?

example:
¿Qué coño es esto? Te dije que no tuvieras una fiesta en la casa.

translation:
What the hell is this? I told you not to have a party at home.

SYNONYM -1: **¿Qué carajos es esto?** *exp*. *(Mexico)*.

SYNONYM -2: **¿Qué cojones es esto?** *exp*. • (lit.): What balls is this?

SYNONYM -3: **¿Qué chingado es esto?** *exp.* *(Mexico)* • (lit.): What the fuck is this?

SYNONYM -4: **¿Qué diablos es esto?** *exp.* *(Mexico)* • (lit.): What devils is this?

¡Siéntate, coño! *interj* For God's sake, sit down! • (lit.): Sit down, cunt!

example:
¡Siéntate coño! ¡Andar para arriba y para abajo no va a resolver nada!

translation:
For God's sake, sit down! Pacing back and forth isn't going to solve anything!

SYNONYM: **¡Siéntate, buey/guey!** *interj.* *(Mexico)*.

A CLOSER LOOK -1:
The Many Uses of "Coño"

The term *coño* is a widely used word in many Spanish-speaking countries. The original connotation of *coño* was extremely strong and vulgar, meaning "vagina," or more closely, "cunt." Over the years, it has lost its original meaning and is now used in a variety of expressions. (As mentioned earlier, the term *coño* is not used in Mexico. Therefore, in the following expressions, the term *buey*, literally meaning "ox" would replace *coño* when referring to a person, and *carajo* when referring to a thing or situation.)

¿Adónde coño vas? *exp.*
Where the hell are you going?

MEXICO: **¿Adóne carajo vas?** *exp.*

coña *f.* • **1.** vagina • **2.** joking.

NOTE: This is a variation of the masculine noun *coño* meaning "vagina."

ALSO -1: **¡No me des la coña!** *interj.* Fuck off! • (lit.): Don't give me the cunt!

ALSO -2: **de coña** *exp.* (Spain) by pure luck • *Conseguí este trabajo de coña;* I got this job by pure luck.

coñazo (ser un) *n.* to be a pain-in-the-neck.

NOTE: This is a variation of the masculine noun *coño* meaning "vagina."

coñazo *m.* horrible boredom • *¡Qué coñazo!;* What boredom!

coño *m.* **1.** a fucking idiot • **2.** vagina • (lit.): cunt.

el coño de la Bernarda *exp.* a real mess • (lit.): Bernarda's cunt.

MEXICO: **el buey de la Bernarda** *exp.*

¡El coño de tu madre! *interj. (Cuba)* Fuck your mother! • (lit.): The cunt of your mother!

MEXICO: **¡El carajo de tu madre!** *interj.*

¡Me cago en el recontracoño de tu reputísima madre! *exp.* *(Cuba – extremely vulgar)* Fuck you! • (lit.): I shit on the super cunt of your super whore mother!

¿Qué coño? *exp.* What the hell?

MEXICO: **¿Qué carajo?** *exp.*

¿Qué coño es esto? *exp.* What the hell is this?

MEXICO: **¿Qué carajo es esto?** *exp.*

¿Qué coño quieres? *exp.* What the hell do you want?

MEXICO: **¿Qué carajo quieres?** *exp.*

¿Quién coño viene? *exp.* Who the hell is coming?

MEXICO: **¿Quién carajo viene?** *exp.*

quinto coño (estar en el)
exp. to be somewhere very far
• (lit.): to be in the fifth cunt.

quinto coño (ir al) *exp.* to go
somewhere far away, to go to
the boonies • (lit.): fifth cunt
(to go to the).

**¡Vete al coño de tu
madre!** *interj.* Fuck you!
• (lit.): Go to your mother's
cunt!

MEXICO: **¡Vete al carajo
de tu madre!** *interj.*

A CLOSER LOOK -2:

The Many Uses of "Culo"

(meaning "buttocks" or "ass")

besa mi culo *exp.* kiss my ass.
VARIATION: **bésame el
culo**.

culear *v.* to fornicate.
NOTE: This comes from the
masculine noun *culo* meaning
"ass."

culero *m.* **1.** a drug thief who
smuggles drugs by hiding them
in the rectum (from the
masculine noun *culo* meaning
"ass") • **2.** homosexual, "fag" •
3. brown-noser.

culo (estar de) *exp.* to feel
out of sorts • (lit.): to be like
an asshole.

**culo mal asiento (estar
un)** *exp.* to be fidgety
• (lit.): to have an ass that
won't sit right.

culón *m.* one with a big ass.

dar candela por el culo
exp. (Cuba) to take it up the
ass • (lit.): to give fire up the
ass.

dar por [el] culo *exp.* to butt-fuck • (lit.): to give through the ass.

encular *v.* to butt-fuck • (lit.): to enter the *culo* meaning "ass."

ir con el culo a rastras *exp.* • **1.** to be in a jam • **2.** to be broke • (lit.): to go with the ass dragging.

ir de culo *exp.* to go downhill, to deteriorate • (lit.): to go on its ass.

¡Jódete y aprieta el culo! *exp. (Cuba)* Go fuck yourself! • (lit.): Fuck you and hold your ass tight!

lameculos *n.* ass-kisser • (lit.): ass-licker.

lamer el culo de alguien *exp.* to kiss up to someone • (lit.): to lick someone's ass.

¡Métetelo por el culo! *exp.* Shove it up your ass! • (lit.): Put it in your ass!

ojo del culo *m.* anal sphincter • (lit.): eye of the ass.

¡Vete por ahí a que te den por el culo! *interj.* Fuck you! • (lit.): Go where you'll get it up the ass!

LECCIÓN DIEZ - The Many Uses of "Chingar" & "Joder"

¿Has conocido ya al nuevo empleado? *¡Me chinga!*

(trans.): Have you met the new employee?
He fucking bugs me!
(lit.): Have you met the new employee?
He fucks me!

Lección Diez · Dialogue in Slang

Enrique: ¿Has conocido ya al nuevo empleado? ¡**Chingao**! ¡Es un **chingado idiota**! ¡**Me la chinga**!

Manuel: Sí, estoy de acuerdo. Ese **chingado** le dijo al jefe que yo llegué diez minutos tarde, para que me **chingue**. Si hace eso otra vez, lo voy a decir que se vaya a **joder por ahí**.

Enrique: ¡**Qué jodida**! ¡**Hijo de su chingada madre**! ¡**Qué se joda**! Este tipo ya me es una **jodienda**. Y no te puedes creer el trabajo **tan jodido** que hace.

Manuel: **Hay que joderse**. ¡A lo mejor le despiden!

Have you met the new employee? He fucking bugs me!

Enrique: Have you met the new employee? **Fuck**! He's such a **fucking idiot**! He really **fucking bugs me**!

Manuel: I know what you mean. That **fucker** told the boss that I got to work ten minutes late which really **bugs the fuck out of me**. If he does that again, I'm going to tell him **to go to to hell**.

Enrique: **Fuck! What an asshole! He can go fuck himself**! This guy's a **fucking pain-in-the-ass**. And you wouldn't believe the **fucked up** job that he's doing here.

Manuel: **To hell with it all**! Maybe he'll get himself fired!

Vocabulary

chingado/a *n. & adj.* fucker; fucking annoying • (lit.): fucker.

example:
Ese **chingado** va a pagar por lo que me hizo.

translation:
That **fucker** is going to pay for what he did to me.

SYNONYM: **jodido/a** *n. & adj.* • (lit.): fucked.

chingado idiota *m.* fucking idiot • (lit.): fucked idiot.

example:
Ese **chingado idiota** no sabe que lleva la cremallera abierta.

translation:
That **fucking idiot** doesn't know his zipper is open.

NOTE: In Mexico, *pinche idiota* is used instead.

chingar *v.* • **1.** to bug the fuck out of someone • **2.** to fuck • (lit.): to fuck.

example -1:
Ese tipo me está siempre **chingando**.

translation:
That guy is always **bugging the fuck out of me**.

example -2:
¿Cómo te atreves a decirme eso? ¡**Chíngate**!

translation:
How dare you do that to me? **Fuck you**!

SYNONYM: **joder** *v.* • (lit.): to fuck.

¡Chingao! *interj*. Fuck! • (lit.): Fucked!

example:
¡Chingao! No tengo ganas de trabajar hoy.

translation:
Fuck! I don't feel like working today.

NOTE: This is a common pronunciation in Puerto Rico and Cuba where the ending *-ado* is typically pronounced *–ao*. For example: *tirado* ("pulled") = **tira_o_** • *cansado* ("tired") = **cans_ao_**, etc.

¡Hay que joderse! *interj*. To hell with it all! • (lit.): One has to get fucked!

example:
Bueno, ¡**hay que joderse**! Me doy por vencido.

translation:
Well, **to hell with it all**! I give up.

SYNONYM: **¡Hay que chingarse!** *exp*. • (lit.): One has to get fucked!

¡Hijo de su chingada madre! *interj*. What an asshole! • (lit.): Son of his fucked mother!

example:
¡Hijo de su chingada madre! Siempre tengo que terminar su trabajo.

translation:
What an asshole! I always have to finish his work.

ir a joder por ahí *exp*. to go to hell • (lit.): to go and fuck somewhere else.

example:
¿Por qué no te **vas a joder por ahí**? ¡Ya me estás agobiando!

translation:
Why don't you **go to hell**? You're annoying me!

jodiendo/a *n.* a fucking pain-in-the-ass • (lit.): to be a fuck.

example:
Mi hermana quiere que la recoga en el aeropuerto en hora punta.
¡Qué **jodienda**!

translation:
My sister wants me to pick her up at the airport during rush hour.
What **a fucking pain-in-the-ass**!

¡Me chinga! *interj.* He really fucking bugs me! • (lit.): He fucks me over!

example:
¡Mi nuevo jefe **me chinga**! ¡El siempre critica todo lo que hago!

translation:
My new boss really **fucking bugs me**! He keeps criticizing everything I do!

¡Qué jodida! *interj.* fuck! • (lit.): Fuck!

example:
¡**Joder**! ¡Qué calor hace hoy!

translation:
Fuck! It's hot today!

SYNONYM -1: **¡Chingao¡** *interj.* • (lit.): Fuck!

SYNONYM -2: **¡En la madre!** *exp. (Mexico)* • In the mother!

¡Qué se joda! *interj.* Fuck him! • (lit.): May he fuck himself!

example:
¡**Qué se joda**! Yo no le voy a ayudar más.

translation:
Fuck him! I'm not going to help him anymore.

SYNONYM: **¡Qué se chingue!** *interj.* • (lit.): Fuck him!

tan jodido/a *adj*. totally fucked up • (lit.): so fucked up.

example:
Mi hermana me ayudó a pintar la casa pero hizo un trabajo **tan jodido**. ¡Deberías ver lo que hizo a la fachada de la casa!

translation:
My sister helped me paint my house but she did a **totally fucked up** job. You should see what she did to the front of the house!

SYNONYM: tan chingado/a *exp*. • (lit.): so fucked up.

A CLOSER LOOK -1:
The Many Uses of "Chingar"
(primarily used in Mexico)

¡A la chingada! *exp*. Fuck it!

¡Chinga tu madre! *exp*. Fuck you! • (lit.): Fuck your mother!

chingado/a [noun] *adj*. fucking [noun] (i.e. *chingado idiota*; fucking idiot).

¡Chingao! *interj*. Fuck!

chingar *v*. **1.** to fuck • **2.** to cheat • **3.** to tire someone • **4.** to annoy.

chingar a alguien *v*. to bug the shit out of someone.

chingón *m*. fucker (from the verb *chingar* meaning "to fuck").

NOTE: This term is also used in reference to a person who is very good at something. For example: *Carlos en un chingón en matemáticas;* Carlos is fucking good at math.

¡Hijo de su chingada madre! *exp*. You son of a bitch! • (lit.): Son of your fucked mother!

A CLOSER LOOK -2:
The Many Uses of "Joder"

¡Hay que joderse! *exp.* To hell with everything! • (lit.): One should fuck oneself!

joda *f.* • **1.** nuisance • *Esto es una joda*; This is a nuisance • **2.** joke • *Alfonso me dijo una buena joda*; Alfonso told me a good joke.

¡Joder! *interj.* Fuck! (used to denote anger, surprise, disappointment) • *¡Joder! ¡Dejame en paz!*; Fuck! Leave me alone!

joder *v.* • **1.** to fuck • **2.** to annoy • **3.** to steal • **4.** to fuck up • **5.** failure, flop.

joderse *v.* to be annoying • *Esto me jode*; This is annoying me.

¡Jódete y aprieta el culo! *exp. (Cuba)* Go fuck yourself! • (lit.): Fuck you and hold tight your ass!

jodido/a *adj.* • **1.** exhausted, wiped out • *Después de trabajar todo el fin de semana, estoy jodido*; After working all weekend I'm wiped out. •

2. difficult • *Yo creo que el examen era muy jodido*; I think the test was very difficult. • **3.** fucking • *¡Guillermo es un jodido idiota!*; Guillermo is such a fucking idiot! • **4.** ruined • *¡Derramé jugo de tomate en mi chaleco nuevo y lo jodí!*; I spilled tomato juice on my new sweater and ruined it! • **5.** destitute, broke • *Clarissa perdió un montón de dinero en las apuestas; Ahora está jodida*; Clarissa lost all of her money gambling. Now she's broke. • (lit.): fucked.

jodido/a pero contento/a *exp.* a common response to someone asking how you're doing • (lit.): fucked but content.

jodienda *f.* annoying person or thing, pain-in-the-ass • (lit.): act of fucking.

jodón/ona *n. & adj.* pain-in-the-ass; fucking annoying.

jodontón/ona n. & adj.
"horndog"; sexual, horny.

¡Qué te jodas! interj. Fuck
off! • (lit.): May you fuck
yourself!

¡No me jodas! exp. Don't fuck
around with me! • (lit.): Don't
fuck me!

¡Vete a joder por ahí!
interj. Fuck off! • (lit.): Go
fuck over there!

A CLOSER LOOK -3:
Drug Slang

When I was in junior high school, another student offered me a
cigarette containing a substance he called "elephant tranquilizer."
Having never smoked and not being familiar with this slang expression,
I refused it. Later I learned that "elephant tranquilizer" is a slang term
for a drug called "phencyclidine" or "PCP," a dangerous drug that has
been known to cause violent behavior or death.

Knowing the following drug terms will help any unsuspecting victim to
recognize and avoid a potentially hazardous situation.

acostarse con rosemaria
exp. (Mexico) to smoke
marijuana • (lit.): to go to bed
with Rosemary.

aracata f. (Mexico) marijuana.

atizar coliflor tostada exp.
(Mexico) to smoke marijuana
• (lit.): to smoke toasted
cauliflower.

atizar mota exp. (Mexico) to
smoke marijuana • (lit.): to
stir powder.

basuco m. (Mexico, Central
and South America) crack
cocaine.

caballo m. heroin
•(lit.): horse.

chinaloa f. (Mexico) opium, heroin.

chocolate de fu man chu m. (Mexico) opium, heroin
• (lit.): chocolate of fu manchu.

chora f. (Mexico) marijuana.

culero m. (Spain) a drug thief who smuggles drugs by hiding them in the rectum (from the masculine noun culo meaning "ass").

grifear v. (Mexico) to smoke marijuana.

grifo m. (Mexico) drug addict
• (lit.): faucet, tap.

grilla f. (Mexico, Central and South America) marijuana
• (lit.): female cricket.

gumersinda f. heroin or opium.

hierba f. (Mexico) marijuana
• (lit.): grass or herb.
NOTE: Also spelled: yerba.

lina f. (Mexico) line of cocaine
• (lit.): line.

llello m. (Mexico, Puerto Rico) cocaine, crack.

malva f. (Mexico) marijuana
• (lit.): mallow.

mary f. (Mexico) marijuana.

mastuerzo m. (Mexico) marijuana.

moravia f. (Mexico) marijuana.

morisqueta f. (Mexico) marijuana • (lit.): speck.

mota f. (Mexico).

motivosa f. (Mexico) marijuana.
NOTE: This is a variation of the masculine noun motivo meaning "motive" or "reason."

motocicleta f. (Mexico) marijuana • (lit.): motor-cycle.

motor de chorro m. (Mexico) marijuana
• (lit.): jet engine.

motorizar *v. (Mexico, Central and South America)* to smoke marijuana • (lit.): to motorize.

nalga de angel *f. (Mexico)* marijuana • (lit.): buttocks of an angel.

orégano *m. (Mexico)* marijuana • (lit.): oregano.

orégano chino *m. (Mexico)* marijuana • (lit.): Chinese oregano.

perico *m. (Mexico, Central and South America)* cocaine • (lit.): periwig.

verde *f.* marijuana • (lit.): green.

zacate inglés *m. (Mexico and Central America)* marijuana • (lit.): English hay.

A CLOSER LOOK -4:
Being Obscene Unintentionally
(and other embarrassing moments)

Americans naturally assume that when they go to another English-speaking country like England, for example, they will certainly have no problem communicating and will be readily understood. However, the unsuspecting traveler learns quickly that this is *not* the case.

As an American, if you ask an English hotel or innkeeper where the restroom is, you'll undoubtedly evoke a confused response of, "But sir, you're standing in it!" Hmmmm. Looks like an awfully fancy bathroom. Perhaps he didn't quite understand. No problem. Simply rephrase the question and ask for the bathroom. "Oh! Yes, of course, sir! Just down that corridor." Finally! You've made yourself understood...or have you? When you open the door to the bathroom and all you see is just that...a bath, you'll quickly realize that something is wrong because in England the bathroom is referred to as the toilet and the bath is in a separate room altogether, the bathroom.

In Spanish, the speaker has to be concerned with many different Spanish-speaking countries, which dramatically increases the chance for innocent blunders of this sort.

In this section, you'll see a sentence in Spanish followed by the different possible translations that it can have depending on context or country.

As shown in the first example, you'll see that if a native of Spain asks a native of Argentina where to catch the bus, the Argentinean may stand there stunned for a moment, then run away!

¿Dónde puedo coger el autobús?

Common Translation:
          Where can I catch the bus?

Translation in Argentina / Chile / Mexico:
          Where can I fuck the bus?

NOTE: In Argentina and Chile, these are the preferred ways to say, "Where can I catch the bus?"

• ¿Dónde puedo agarrar *(to grab, to seize)* el autobús?

• ¿Dónde puedo tomar *(to take)* el autobús?

• ¿Dónde puedo pillar *(to catch)* el autobús?

• ¿Dónde puedo recoger *(to pick up, to gather, to fetch)* el autobús?

¿Quieres que te fría un huevo?

Common Translation #1:
          Would you like me to fry you an egg?

Common Translation #2:
          Would you like me to fry one of your testicles?

¿Te gusta la papaya?

Common Translation:
> Do you like papaya?

Translation in Cuba / Puerto Rico / Dominican Republic
> Do you like vagina?

NOTE: In Cuba, *papaya* is referred to as *fruta bomba* or "puffed-out fruit."

Conoces a ese individuo?

Common Translation:
> Do you know that guy?

Translation in Argentina:
> Do you know that weird person?

NOTE: In Argentina, the masculine noun *individuo* should be used with caution since it is insulting.

Conozco a ese pájaro.

Translation in Chile / Peru / Ecuador:
> I know that guy.

Translation in Cuba / Puerto Rico / Dominican Republic
> I know that homosexual.

Voy a la playa a buscar almejas.

Common Translation #1:
> I go to the beach to look for clams.

Common Translation #2:
> I go to the beach to look for vagina.

Cuando veo un bicho lo pisoteo.

Common Translation #1:
> Whenever I see a bug, I squash it.

Common Translation #2:
> Whenever I see a penis, I squash it.

Este restaurante tiene los mejores bollos.

Common Translation:
> This restaurant has the best bread rolls.

Translation in Cuba:
> This restaurant has the best vagina.

Voy a la playa a buscar conchas.

Common Translation:
> I go to the beach to look for seashells.

Translation in Mexico:
> I go to the beach to look for vagina.

Mi madre me va a comprar un conejo para mi cumpleaños.

Common Translation:
> My mother's going to buy me a rabbit for my birthday.

Translation in Mexico:
> My mother's going to buy me a vagina for my birthday.

Me comí un chorizo entero a la hora del desayuno.

Common Translation #1:
>   I ate a whole pork sausage for breakfast.

Common Translation #2:
>   I ate a whole penis for breakfast.

¡Mira! Ese hombre está vendiendo churros.

Common Translation:
>   Look! That man's selling fritters!

Common Translation in Mexico:
>   Look! That man's selling penises!

¡Qué follón tan horrible!

Common Translation:
>   What a horrible mess!

Translation in Mexico:
>   What a horrible fart!

Vamos a coger mariposas.

Common Translation:
>   We're going to catch butterflies.

Translation in Argentina / Chile / Mexico
>   We're going to fuck homosexuals.

¡Esos melocotones son enormes!

Common Translation:
> Those peaches are enormous!

Translation in Mexico:
> Those boobs are enormous!

Creo que venden nabos en este mercado.

Common Translation #1:
> I think they sell turnips in this market.

Common Translation #2:
> I think they sell penises in this market.

Le echó un palo a su perro.

Common Translation #1:
> He threw his dog a stick.

Common Translation #2:
> He fucked his dog.

NOTE: **echar un palo** *exp.* to screw, copulate with • (lit.): to throw a stick.

¿Soplaste ese pito?

Common Translation #1:
> Did you blow that whistle?

Common Translation #2:
> Did you blow that penis?

Sirvieron el bistec con una seta grande encima.

Common Translation:
> They served the steak with a big mushroom on top.

Translation in Mexico:
> They served the steak with a big vagina on top.

Es mi tortillera favorita.

Common Translation #1:
> She's my favorite tortilla vendor.

Common Translation #2:
> She's my favorite lesbian.

Esta sopa tiene muchos zurullos.

Common Translation #1:
> This soup has a lot of lumps in it.

Common Translation #2:
> This soup has a lot of turds in it.

¡Qué vista tan bella desde este pico!

Common Translation #1:
> What a beautiful view from this peak!

Common Translation #2:
> What a beautiful view from this penis!

Mi hermana cría pollas.

Common Translation #1:
> My sister raises young hens.

Common Translation #2:
> My sister raises penises.

Voy a la tienda a comprar una cajetilla.

Common Translation:
> I'm going to the store to buy a pack of cigarettes.

Translation in Argentina / Uruguay:
> I'm going to the store to buy a homosexual.

Mi chucha acaba de parir.

Common Translation:
> My female dog just had babies.

Translation in Chile:
> My vagina just had babies.

Mi padre me regaló un coche para mi cumpleaños.

Common Translation:
> My father gave me a car for my birthday.

Translation in Guatemala:
> My father gave me a pig for my birthday.

Estoy muy embarazada.

Mistaken Translation:
> I'm very embarrassed.

Actual Translation:
> I'm very pregnant.

Necesito una chaqueta.

Common Translation:
> I need a jacket.

Translation in Mexico:
> I need a hand-job.

GLOSSARY

A

a cuatro patas *exp.* doggie-style • (lit.): on all four paws.

¡A la chingada! *exp.* Fuck it!

¡A la puñeta! *interj.* *(Cuba)* Go to hell! • (lit.): Go to masturbation!

¡A la verga! *intjer.* Fuck it! • (lit.): To the penis!

a lo perro *adv.* doggie-style • (lit.): in the style of a dog.

abadesa *f.* *(Mexico)* pimp • (lit.): head of the house.

acabar *v.* *(Argentina)* to ejaculate, to have an orgasm • (lit.): to finish • *¡Estoy por acabar!;* I'm going to ejaculate!

acariciar *v.* • (lit.): to caress, touch lightly.

acariciarse *v.* to masturbate • (lit.): to fondle oneself.

aceite *n. & adj.* *(Cuba)* tightwad; stingy • (lit.): oil.

acostarse con rosemaria *exp.* *(Mexico)* to smoke marijuana • (lit.): to go to bed with Rosemary.

¿Adónde coño vas? *exp.* Where the hell are you going? **MEXICO:** **¿Adóne carajo vas?** *exp.*

adoquín *adj.* *(Cuba)* idiot • (lit.): paving stone.

aduana *f.* *(Mexico)* whorehouse • (lit.): Customs.

afeminado *m.* homosexual • (lit.): an effeminate [man].

agarraderas *f.pl.* *(Mexico)* breasts, "tits" • (lit.): grabbers (from the verb *agarrar* meaning "to take" or "to grab").

agarrado/a *n. & adj.* tightwad; stingy • (lit.): held.

aguacates *m.pl.* *(Mexico)* testicles • (lit.): little avocados.

albondigas *f.pl. (Mexico)* testicles • (lit.): meatballs.

alcahuete *m.* pimp • (lit.): wild artichoke.

alcaucil *m.* pimp • (lit.): wild artichoke.

alforjas *m.pl.* testicles • (lit.): saddlebags.

alimentos *m.pl. (Mexico)* "tits" • (lit.): **1.** food allowance • **2.** alimony.

almeja *f. (extremely vulgar)* vagina, "cunt" • (lit.): clam.

VARIATION: almejilla *f.* • (lit.): small clam.

alzado/a *n. & adj.* snob; stuck up • (lit.): from the verb *alzar* meaning "to lift" which refers to a snobby person's nose in the air.

amaricado • **1.** *m.* homosexual, "fag" • **2.** *adj.* effeminate.

amaricarse *v.* to become homosexual (from the masculine noun *maricón* meaning "fag").

amor a primera vista *exp.* love at first sight • (lit.): [same].

andar con el estómaco flojo *exp. (Mexican)* to have diarrhea • (lit.): to walk around with a loose stomach..

andar con mal tapón *exp. (Mexican)* to be constipated • (lit.): to walk around with a defective cork.

andar con otra *exp.* to have more then one girlfriend • (lit.): to walk with another female.

andar con otro *exp.* to have more than one boyfriend • (lit.): to walk with another male.

angel custodio *m. (Mexico)* condom • (lit.): guardian angel.

angel de la guardia *m. (Mexico)* condom • (lit.): guardian angel.

aparato *m. (Mexico)* penis, "dick" • (lit.): apparatus.

apestar la boca *exp.* to have bad breath • (lit.): to stink from the mouth.

apestar *v.* to stink • (lit.): to infect with the plague.

VARIATION: apestar a muertos *exp.* to stink to high heaven • (lit.): to stink to death.

ALSO: peste *f.* stink, foul smell • (lit.): plague, epidemic disease • *¡Qué peste!;* What a horrible smell!

aplomado/a *n. & adj.* lazy bum; lazy • (lit.): serious, solemn.

apretado/a *n. & adj. (Mexico)* tightwad; stingy • (lit.): squashed, tightly-packed.

aracata *f. (Mexico)* marijuana.

aragán *n. & adj.* lazy bum; lazy.

ardilla *f. (Puerto Rico)* prostitute • (lit.): squirrel.

argolla *f.* vagina, "pussy" • (lit.): ring, hoop, band.

argolluda/o de mierda *n.* an insult for a woman • (lit.): big ring of shit (referring to her anus).

arma *f.* penis, "dick" • (lit.): weapon.

armado (estar) *adj.* to get an erection • (lit.): to be armed.

arrastrado/a *n. & adj.* lazy bum; lazy. • (lit.): wretched, miserable.

arrecho *adj.* (*Peru, Ecuador*) horny • (lit.): sexually excited.

arrimarse *v.* to get married, to tie the knot • (lit.): to shelve oneself (and be in circulation no longer).

asentaderas *f.pl.* seat, buttocks • (lit.): from the verb *asentar* meaning "to seat."

asqueroso/a *n. & adj.* jerk, disgusting person; jerky • (lit.): filthy.

atar el nudo *exp.* to get married, to tie the knot • (lit.): to tie the knot.

atizar coliflor tostada *exp.* (*Mexico*) to smoke marijuana • (lit.): to smoke toasted cauliflower.

atizar mota *exp.* (*Mexico*) to smoke marijuana • (lit.): to stir powder.

¡Ay que la chingada! *interj.* Oh, shit!

ayotes *m.pl.* (*Mexico*) testicles • (lit.): pumpkins.

baboso/a *n. & adj.* • idiot; stupid (lit.): one who dribbles a lot.

bacán *m.* (*Argentina, Uruguay*) lazy bum.

bacalao *m.* (*Mexico*) vagina, "pussy" • (lit.): codfish.

bajar al pozo *exp.* (*Cuba*) to eat pussy • (lit.): to go down to the well.

bandera roja *f.* menstruation • (lit.): red flag.

barrigón/ona de mierda *n.* (*Argentina*) said of someone who is very fat • (lit.): potbelly of shit.

basuco *m.* (*Mexico, Central and South America*) crack cocaine.

bereco/a *n. & adj.* (*El Savador*) idiot; stupid.

berenjena *f.* penis, "dick" • (lit.): eggplant.

berreadero *m.* (*Mexico*) whorehouse • (lit.): a place where one can listen to animals bleat.

besa mi culo *exp.* kiss my ass.
VARIATION: bésame el culo *exp.*

besar con la lengua *exp.* to give a French kiss • (lit.): to kiss with the tongue.

beso *m.* • (lit.): kiss.

beso francés *m.* French kiss • (lit.): [same].

beso negro *m.* a kiss that is applied with the tongue up someone's rectum • (lit.): black kiss.

biberón *m.* penis, "dick" • (lit.): baby bottle, feeding bottle.

bicho *m.* penis, "dick" • (lit.): bug.

bigote *m.* vagina, "pussy" • (lit.): mustache.

bijirita *f.* *(Cuba)* "fag," queer.

bizcocho *m.* vagina, "pussy" • (lit.): sweet bread or sponge cake.

bobo/a *n. & adj.* idiot; stupid • (lit.): foolish.

bocón/ona *n. & adj.* blabbermouth; gossipy • (lit.): big-mouthed.
> **NOTE:** This is from the feminine noun *boca* meaning "mouth."

bofa *n.* crazy woman *(Cuba).*
> **NOTE:** This is from the verb *bofarse* meaning "to sag."

bolas *f.pl.* testicles • (lit.): balls.

bolitas *f.pl.* testicles • (lit.): little balls.

bollaca *f.* lesbian.

bollera *f.* lesbian, "dyke" • (lit.): baker.

bollo *m.* vagina, "pussy" • (lit.): a type of bread.
> **CAUTION:** In western Venezuela, the expression *tremendo bollo* means "nice pussy." However, in other parts of the same country, the expression would simply translate as "big mess" or "fine pickle."

bollo loco *m.* *(Cuba)* an easy lay • (lit.): crazy bread roll or bun.

> **NOTE:** In Cuba, *bollo* ("bread roll" or "bun") is used to refer to "vagina."

bolo *m.* *(Nicaragua, El Salvador)* drunkard • (lit.): skittle.

bonachón/na *n. & adj.* sucker, simpleton; gullible • (lit.): someone who is too nice and good (from the adjective *bueno* meaning "good").

borrachal *m.* drunkard (from the adjective *borracho/a* meaning "drunk").

borrachón/ona *f. & adj.* *(Argentina)* severe drunkard • (lit.): big drunkard.

bosta *f.* turd, cow dung • (lit.): cow dung.

botarse la cantúa *exp. (Cuba)* to masturbate • (lit.): to throw the *cantúa* (a candy made of sweet potato, coconut, sesame, and sugar).

botarse la puñeta *exp. (Cuba)* to masturbate • (lit.): to throw the cuff.

botarse la yuca *exp. (Cuba)* to masturbate • (lit.): to throw the yucca plant.

botarse una paja *exp. (Cuba)* to masturbate • (lit.): to toss a straw.

botija *n. & adj.* fat slob; chunky, fat • (lit.): short-necked earthen jug.

broca *f.* penis, "dick" • (lit.): the bit of a drill.

bruja *f.* whore • (lit.): witch.

bruquena *f.* vagina, "pussy."

bruto/a de mierda *n.* (*Argentina*) idiot • (lit.): brute of shit.

buche *n. & adj.* (*Cuba*) idiot; crazy • (lit.): mouthful.

buenona *f.* (*Spain*) beautiful girl, hot chick.

NOTE: This is from the feminine adjective *buena* meaning "good."

buey *m. & adj.* idiot; stupid • (lit.): ox, bullock.

bufa *f.* • **1.** (*Cuba*) drunkard • **2.** fart.

bufete *m.* buttocks, ass • (lit.): **1.** writing desk • **2.** lawyer's office.

bufo *m.* homosexual, "fag" • (lit.): clownish, comic.

bujarrón *m.* homosexual, "fag" • (lit.): sodomite.

burro/a *n. & adj.* jerk; crazy. • (lit.): donkey.

NOTE: In Mexico, the term **burro/a** is also used to mean "a bad student."

buscar flete *exp.* (*Cuba*) to look for some ass • (lit.): to look for freight, cargo.

buscona *f.* prostitute • (lit.): one who searches (from the verb *buscar* meaning "to search").

butifarra *f.* penis, "dick" • (lit.): pork sausage.

C

¡Cállate! *interj.* Shut up! • (lit.): Shut yourself!

¡Cállate/Cierra el hocico! *interj.* Shut up! • (lit.): Shut your mouth!

NOTE: **hocico** *m.* • (lit.): the mouth of an animal (and derogatory when used in reference to a person).

¡Cállate/Cierra el pico! *exp.* Shut your trap! • (lit.): Shut your beak!

¡Cállate/Cierra la boca! *exp.* Shut your mouth! • (lit.): Close your mouth!

cáncamo *m.* (*Cuba*) ugly man • (lit.): louse.

cántaros *m.pl.* breasts • (lit.): pitcher, wine measure.

caballo *m.* heroin • (lit.): horse.

caballo *m.* tampon • (lit.): horse.

cabrón/ona *n. & adj.* asshole; jerky • (lit.): billy-goat.

VARIATION: **re-cabrón** *m.* (*Argentina*) a big asshole.

NOTE: In Argentina, the prefix *re-* is commonly added to many words to add greater emphasis.

cachapera *f.* (*Puerto Rico, Venezuela*) lesbian, "dyke."

NOTE: This comes from the feminine term *cachapa* which is a thin pancake, usually served stacked. Therefore, a stack of *cachapas* conjures up the image of several vaginas stacked one on top of the other.

NOTE: cachapear *v.* to engage in lesbian sex • *Ellas se estaban cachapeando;* They're having lesbian sex.

cachar *v. (Peru)* to have sex, to fornicate • (lit.): to break into pieces.

cachas *f.pl.* buttocks • (lit.): cheeks (of face).

cachetes *m.pl.* buttocks • (lit.): cheeks (of face).

cachetes del culo *m.pl.* buttocks • (lit.): cheeks of the ass.

cacho *m. (El Salvador)* penis, "dick" • (lit.): small piece, chunk.

cafiche *m. (Chile)* pimp.

caficio *m. (Argentina)* pimp.

cagada *f.* shit (from the verb *cagar* meaning "to shit").

ALSO -1: hacer una cagada a alguien *exp.* to do something nasty to someone.

ALSO -2: cagada (una) *f. (Argentina)* said of something unpleasant • (lit.): a shit.

cagón/ona *n. & adj.* coward, scared • (lit.): one who is scared shitless.

cagadero *m.* bathroom, "shithouse" (from the verb *cagar* meaning "to shit").

cagado/a (estar) *adj.* to be full of shit • (lit.): to be shit.

cagado/a de miedo (estar) *exp.* to be scared shitless • (lit.): to be shit with fear.

cagar *v.* • **1.** to defecate • **2.** to make a mistake • (lit.): to shit.

cagarse de gusto *exp.* to enjoy something very much • (lit.): to shit oneself with pleasure.

cagarse en alguien o algo *exp.* to curse someone or something • (lit.): to shit on someone or something.

cagarse en los pantalones *exp.* to be scared shitless • (lit.): to shit in one's pants (due to fear).

cagarse por las patas abajo *exp.* to be scared to death • (lit.): to shit in one's pants.

cagitis (tener) *exp.* to have diarrhea • (lit.): to have the shits.

¡Cago en tu leche! *interj.* Fuck you! • (lit.): I shit in your milk!

cajeta *f. (Argentina)* vagina, "pussy" • (lit.): a type of sweet pudding.

calabazo *m. (Mexico)* buttocks • (lit.): squash, pumpkin, marrow.

calado/a *adj.* moist • (lit.): soaking wet.

calcetín *m.* condom • (lit.): sock.

calcetines con canicas *m.pl.* sagging breasts • (lit.): socks with marbles.

calco *m.* bald • (lit.): tracing (drawing).

calentorro/a *adj.* horny.

NOTE: This is a variation of the adjective *caliente* meaning "hot."

calienta culos *f.* prostitute • (lit.): ass warmer.

calientapollas *n. & adj. (Spain)* prick teaser • (lit.): one who makes a penis (*polla*, literally "young chicken") hot (*caliente*).

caliente *adj.* horny, sexually hot • (lit.): hot.

callejera *f.* prostitute • (lit.): pertaining to the street.

calvito *adj.*

NOTE: This is from the adjective *calvo* meaning "bald."

cambiarle el agua al canario *exp.* to urinate • (lit.): to change the canary's water.

camote *m.* penis, "dick" • (lit.): sweet potato.

canario *m.* penis, "dick" • (lit.): canary.

caoba *f. (Cuba)* penis, "dick" • (lit.): mahogany tree.

capucha *f.* condom • (lit.): hood (of a garment).

capuchón *m.* condom • (lit.): hood (of a garment).

capullo *m.* bastard, asshole • (lit.): bud or head of the penis.

carajo *m.* penis, "dick" • (lit.): penis.

NOTE: This term is commonly used in Mexico as an expletive. For example: *¡Carajo!*; Shit!

carallo *m.* penis, "dick."

NOTE: This is a variation of the masculine noun *carajo* meaning "penis."

carapedo *m.* stupid, fart-face • (lit.): fart-face.

caricia *f.* caress • (lit.): caress.

casa de citas *f.* whorehouse • (lit.): a house where one can have a date.

casa de putas *f.* whorehouse • (lit.): house of whores.

casado con la viuda de los cinco hijos (estar) *exp.* *(Cuba)* to masturbate • (lit.): to be married to the widow of the five children.

casco *m.* ugly woman • (lit.): helmet.

casita de paja *f. (Puerto Rico)* vagina, "pussy" • (lit.): small house of straw.

casquete (echar un) *exp.* to have a fuck • (lit.): to throw a helmet.

cataplines *m.* testicles.

cebollín *m. (Cuba)* stupid person • (lit.): small onion.

cebollón *m. (Cuba)* stupid person • (lit.): large onion.

cepillar *v.* to fornicate • (lit.): to brush.

VARIATION: **cepillarse a** *v.*

cepillo *m.* vagina, "pussy" • (lit.): brush.

cerote m. (*Nicaragua*) turd • (lit.): large zero.

ciendango m. *Cuba*) homosexual, "fag."

cipote m. penis, "dick" • (lit.): silly, foolish.

clavar v. to fornicate • (lit.): to nail.

coña f. • **1.** vagina • **2.** joking.

NOTE: This is a variation of the masculine noun *coño* meaning "vagina."

ALSO -1: ¡No me des la coña! *interj.* Fuck off! • (lit.): Don't give me the cunt!

ALSO -2: de coña *exp.* (*Spain*) by pure luck • *Conseguí este trabajo de coña;* I got this job by pure luck.

coñazo (ser un) n. • **1.** to be a pain-in-the-neck • **2.** to be a horrible bore • **3.** to be a fucking idiot.

NOTE: This is a variation of the masculine noun *coño* meaning "vagina."

coño m. vagina, "cunt."

NOTE: This term is commonly used in many Spanish-countries (with the exception of Mexico) as an interjection denoting surprise, anger, or annoyance. For example: *¡Coño! ¡No sabía que iba a llover!;* Shit! I didn't know it was supposed to rain!

cobo m. (*Puerto Rico*) old whore • (lit.): gigantic snail.

cocho m. (*Mexico, El Salvador*) vagina, "pussy" • (lit.): dirty, filthy.

cochón m. homosexual, "fag."

codo m. & adj. tightwad; stingy • (lit.): elbow.

codo empinado m. drunkard • (lit.): tilted elbow.

coger v. to fornicate • (lit.): to get, to catch.

NOTE: This verb leads to many embarrassing moments for natives of Spain who travel to other Spanish-speaking countries. In Spain, the verb *coger* simply means "to catch." It would not be unusual for a Spaniard to travel to Argentina, for example, and ask where he could "catch" the bus by using the phrase: *¿Donde puedo coger el autobús?* translated in Argentina (and many other Spanish-speaking countries) as: "Where can I fuck the bus?"

coger una mierda exp. to get drunk, "shit-faced" • (lit.): to catch a shit.

cogetuda f. (*Argentina*) an easy lay.

NOTE: This is from the verb *coger* meaning (in many Spanish-speaking countries) "to fuck."

cojinetes m. testicles • (lit.): small cushions.

cojones m.pl. testicles, "balls" • (lit.): testicles.

NOTE: The term *cojones* may also be used as an interjection of surprise, anger, or annoyance. Examples: *No me importa dos*

cojones; I don't give a shit • (lit.): I don't care two balls [testicles] about it.
¡Cojones!; Bullshit!
¡Y un cojón!; Like hell it is!
Hace falta tener cojones; You've got to have balls [be brave].
Es un tipo sin cojones; That guy's a coward • (lit.): That guy doesn't have balls [courage].
NOTE: cojonear *v.* to act like a jerk.

cojudo/a *n. & adj.* idiot; stupid • (lit.): uncastrated.

cola *m.* penis, "dick" • (lit.): tail.

colgados *m.pl.* (Mexico) sagging breasts of an old woman • (lit.): hanging things (from the verb *colgar* meaning "to hang").

colgajos *m.pl.* testicles • (lit.): bunch (of fruit).

colgantes *m.pl.* testicles, "balls" • (lit.): "danglers."

comadrera *f.* blabbermouth.
NOTE: This is from the feminine noun *comadre* meaning "gossip."

comebasura *n. & adj.* idiot; stupid • (lit.): garbage-eater.

comelón/ona *n. & adj.* one who eats a lot, pig; piggy.
NOTE: This is from the verb *comer* meaning "to eat."

comemierda *n. & adj.* jerk; jerky • (lit.): shit-eater.

comer *v.* (Peru, Ecuador, Colombia, Chile, Venezuela) to fornicate • (lit.): to eat.

cometer la equivocación *exp.* to get married • (lit.): to make the mistake.

comilón *m.* (Argentina) homosexual, "fag" • (lit.): big eater (of penis).

como bocina de avión (estar/ser) *exp.* (Argentina) to be as useless as a screen door on a submarine • (lit.): to be like a horn in a plane.
VARIATION: inútil como bocina de avión (estar/ser) *exp.* • (lit.): useless as a horn in a plane.

como un cenicero de moto (estar/ser) *exp.* (Argentina) to be totally useless • (lit.): to be like an ashtray on a motorcycle.
VARIATION: inútil como un cenicero de moto (estar/ser) *exp.* • (lit.): to be as useless as an ashtray on a motorcycle.

comprometido/a (estar) *adj.* • (lit.): to be compromised.

concha *f.* (Central America, Cuba, Uruguay, Argentina) vagina, "pussy" • (lit.): sea shell.
ALSO: ¡La concha de tu madre! *interj.* an extremely vulgar insult literally meaning "¡Your mother's cunt!"
VARIATION: concho *m.*

conchudo/a *n. & adj.* lazy bum; lazy.

conejo *m.* vagina, "cunt" • (lit.): rabbit.

congalera f. prostitute, "whore" • (lit.): someone who works at a bordello.

consolador m. dildo • (lit.): comforter, consoler.

corbejo m. (Puerto Rico) old whore.

corchito m. (Argentina) • (lit.): little cork.

corcho m. (El Salvador) annoying person or idiot • (lit.): cork.

correrse v. to ejaculate, to have an orgasm.

NOTE: The intransitive form of this verb *correr* literally means "to run." However, in the reflexive form, it carries a sexual connotation.

cortejo m. (Puerto Rico) pimp • (lit.): escort.

corto/a de mate adj. (Argentina) crazy, touched in the head • (lit.): short in the gourd.

cosita f. penis, "dick" • (lit.): little thing.

cotorra f. blabbermouth • (lit.): parrot.

cotunto/a adj. (Cuba) very ugly.

coyón/na n. & adj. scaredy-cat; scared.

crema f. semen • (lit.): cream.

cretinita f. & adj. (Argentina) idiotic little girl; jerky • (lit.): little cretin.

cretino m. & adj. jerk; jerky • (lit.): cretin.

crica f. (Puerto Rico) vagina, "pussy" • (lit.): vagina.

cua-cua m. (Puerto Rico) homosexual, "fag" (from the sound made by a duck).

cualquiera f. prostitute • (lit.): anyone.

cuarenta y uno m. (Mexico) homosexual male, "fag" • (lit.): forty-one.

NOTE: This expression may have originated since some people think that if you are over forty and you are not married, you might be a homosexual.

cuartito m. bathroom, the "john" • (lit.): small room

cuca f. (Venezuela, El Salvador) vagina, "pussy" • (lit.): clever, smart.

cuchi m. fatso • (lit.): variation of *cochino* meaning "filthy."

cuello duro m. & adj. snob; stuck up • (lit.): hard or stiff neck (from keeping one's nose in the air).

cuentero/a n. & adj. (Argentina) a gossip; gossipy• (lit.): one who tells tales.

cuero m. & adj. • **1.** hunk; hunky • **2.** (Puerto Rico) prostitute who is into leather • (lit.): leather.

cuesco m. fart • (lit.): stone,

cuete (ponerse) adj. to get drunk • (lit.): slice of rump (of beef).

cuevita f. vagina, "pussy" • (lit.): little cave.

culastrón *m.* *(Argentina)* homosexual, "fag."

NOTE: This is a variation of the masculine noun *culo* meaning "ass."

culero *m.* **1.** a drug thief who smuggles drugs by hiding them in the rectum (from the masculine noun *culo* meaning "ass") • **2.** homosexual, "fag" • **3.** brown-noser.

culicagado *m.* little kid • (lit.): shit-covered ass.

culo *m.* ass.

ALSO -1: **culo mal asiento (estar un)** *exp.* to be fidgety • (lit.): to have an ass that won't sit right.

ALSO -2: **culón** *m.* one with a big ass.

ALSO -3: **ir con el culo a rastras** *exp.* • **1.** to be in a jam • **2.** to be broke • (lit.): to go with the ass dragging.

ALSO -4: **ir de culo** *exp.* to go downhill, to deteriorate • (lit.): to go on its ass.

ALSO -5: **lamer el culo de alguien** *exp.* to kiss up to someone • (lit.): to lick someone's ass.

culo (estar de) *exp.* to feel out of sorts • (lit.): to be like an asshole.

culo mal asiento (estar un) *exp.* to be fidgety • (lit.): to have an ass that won't sit right.

culón *m.* one with a big ass.

cundango *m.* homosexual, "fag."

curo *m.* *(Cuba)* penis, "dick" • (lit.): leather strap.

cusca *f.* prostitute, slut • (lit.): prostitute.

cutre *n. & adj.* idiot; stupid.

NOTE: When said of a person, *cutre* means "cheap" or "bad taste." When said of a place, it means "dirty, old, & ugly."

chacón *f.* *(Argentina)* vagina, "pussy" • (lit.): an inversion of the feminine term *concha* meaning "sea shell."

VARIATION: **concho** *m.*

chaira *f.* penis, "dick" • (lit.): cobbler's knife.

champe *m.* *(Cuba)* homosexual male, "fag."

NOTE: This is a variation of the masculine noun *champí* meaning "a tiny insect."

chancho *m.* • (lit.): fat pig.

chango *m.* vagina, "pussy" • (lit.): monkey.

chaparro/a *n. & adj.* runt; runty.

chapero *m.* *(Spain)* male prostitute.

chapete *f.* an easy lay.

chaquetear *v.* to masturbate.

VARIATION: hacer una chaqueta *exp.* to make a jacket.

chava bien [buena] *f.* beautiful girl, hot chick • (lit.): young girl well [good].

chavo bien [bueno] *m.* handsome guy, hunk • (lit.): young guy well [good].

¡Ché dejá de dormir, fiaca de mierda, movéte un poco! *exp.* (Argentina) used in response to seeing a lazy person • (lit.): Hey, stop sleeping, you lazy piece of shit, and move around a little!

¡Ché gordo, te vas a reventar! *exp.* (Argentina) in response to seeing someone very fat • (lit.): Hey fatso, you're going to explode!

¡Chíngate! *interj.* (Mexico) Fuck you! (from the verb *chingar* meaning "to fuck").

chica de alterne *f.* prostitute • (lit.): alternating girl.

chichis *m.pl.* breasts, "tits."

chichona *f.* a woman with big breasts • (lit.): easy, presenting no difficulty.

chicloso *m.* anus • (lit.): made of chewing-gum.

chiflado/a *n. & adj.* crackpot; crazy, nuts • (lit.): whistled (from the verb *chiflar* meaning "to whistle").

chiflo *m.* penis, "dick" • (lit.): whistle.

chile *m.* (Mexico) penis, "dick" • (lit.): chile, hot pepper.

chilito *m.* (Mexico, Spain) an insulting term for a little penis • (lit.): small chile, small hot pepper.

chimba *f.* (Colombia) vagina, "pussy."

NOTE: This is a variation of the masculine noun *chimbo* which is a type of dessert.

chinaloa *f.* (Mexico) opium, heroin.

¡Chinga tu madre! *interj.* Fuck you! • (lit.): Fuck your mother!

¡Chinga tu madre! *interj.* a common insult meaning "Fuck you!" • (lit.): Fuck your mother!

¡Chinga tu madre! *exp.* Fuck you! • (lit.): Fuck your mother!

chingado/a [noun] *adj.* fucking [noun] (i.e. *chingado idiota;* fucking idiot).

¡Chingao! *interj.* Fuck!

chingar a alguien *v.* to bug the shit out of someone.

chingar *v.* **1.** to fuck • **2.** to cheat • **3.** to tire someone • **4.** to annoy.

chingar *v.* to fornicate • (lit.): to fuck.

chingón *m.* fucker (from the verb *chingar* meaning "to fuck").

NOTE: This term is also used in reference to a person who is very good at something. For example: *Carlos en un chingón en matemáticas;* Carlos is fucking good at math.

chiquito *m.* a tiny anus • (lit.): very small, tiny.

chirusa *f. (Argentina)* idiotic little girl • (lit.): ignorant young woman.

chis *m. (Mexico – children's language)* urine, piss.
NOTE: As an interjection, *chis* may be used to mean "shhh!" or "pst!"

chismolero/a *n. & adj.* one who spreads gossip or *chismes;* gossipy.

chismoso/a *n.* one who spreads gossip or *chismes.*

chivo *m.* pimp • (lit.): goat.

chocha *f. (Cuba)* vagina, "pussy" • (lit.): woodcock (a type of game bird).

chocho *m. (Mexico, Spain)* vagina, "pussy" • (lit.): floppy.

chocolate de fu man chu *m.* *(Mexico)* opium, heroin • (lit.): chocolate of fu manchu.

cholo *m. (Mexico, Puerto Rico)* • **1.** pimp • **2.** half-breed, the product of a mixed marriage.

choncha *f.* penis, "dick."

chora *f.* **1.** penis, "dick" • **2.** *(Mexico)* marijuana • (lit.): female thief.

chorizo *m.* penis, "dick" • (lit.): pork sausage.

chorrico *m.* penis, "dick" • (lit.): constant flow or stream.

chucha *f.* vagina, "pussy" • (lit.): bitch dog *(Chile).*

chufle *f.* penis, "dick."

chulo *m. (Spain)* hunk • (lit.): • **1.** bull-fighter's assistant • **2.** pimp.

chumino *m.* vagina, "pussy."

¡Chúpa mi pinga! *interj.* Suck my dick! • (lit.): [same].

¡Chúpa mi polla! *interj.* Suck my dick! • (lit.): Suck my young chicken!

¡Chúpa mi verga! *interj.* Suck my dick! • (lit.): Suck my penis (of an animal).

¡Chúpame, puto! *interj.* Suck my dick, you asshole! Fuck you! • (lit.): Suck me, you faggot!

¡Chúpamela! *interj.* Suck my dick! • (lit.): Suck it!

chupandín *m. (Argentina)* drunkard, lush • (lit.): big sucker (from the verb *chupar* meaning "to suck").

chupar/mamar la pinga *exp.* to give a blow job, to suck dick • (lit.): to suck the "dick."
NOTE: Any slang synonym for "penis" can be used here.

chuparosa *f.* homosexual, "fag."
NOTE: This is a variation of the masculine noun *chupaflor* meaning "humming bird."

chuperson m. (Mexico) penis, "dick."

churro m. • **1.** turd • **2.** penis, "dick" • (lit.): long fritter (churro; a long, straight fried pastry).

> **NOTE -1:** The noun churro is also used to refer to a failure. For example: La película fue un churro; The movie was a bomb.

> **NOTE -2:** In Colombia, a churro means "a sexy guy."

daga f. (Puerto Rico) penis, "dick" • (lit.): dagger.

dar calabazas a alguien exp. to dump someone • (lit.): to give pumpkins to someone.

dar candela por el culo exp. (Cuba) to take it up the ass • (lit.): to give fire up the ass.

dar por donde amarga el pepino exp. to fornicate doggie-style • (lit.): to give where the cucumber is bitter.

dar por [el] culo exp. to butt-fuck • (lit.): to give through the ass.

dar una mamada exp. to give a blow job • (lit.): to give a sucking.

darse el lote exp. (Spain) to kiss, to make out • (lit.): to give each other the portion or allotment (of kisses).

darse una buena calentada exp. (Mexico) to kiss, to make out • (lit.): to give each other a good heating up.

de la acera de enfrente exp. homosexual, "fag" • (lit.): (someone) from the other side of the street.

de la cáscara amarga exp. homosexual, "fag" • (lit.): (someone) from the bitter peel (of fruit)

de la otra acera exp. homosexual, "fag" • (lit.): (someone) from the other side of the street.

de los otros m. homosexual, "fag" • (lit.): one of them.

de mierda adv. said of something lousy or "shitty," for shit • Ese regalo que Pedro me dió el día de mi cumpleaños es de mierda; That gift that Pedro gave me for my birthday was for shit.

de pedo adv. by luck • (lit.): by fart (something that happens as easily as a fart).

de vida fácil exp. said of someone who has an active sex life • (lit.): of an easy (or loose) life.

dejar a alguien exp. to dump someone • (lit.): to leave someone.

dejar a alguien a su suerte exp. to dump someon • (lit.): to leave someone to his/her luck.

dejar clavado/a *exp.* to stand someone up [on a date] • (lit.): to leave nailed (in one place).

dejar plantado/a *exp.* to stand someone up [on a date] • (lit.): to leave planted.

del rejue *exp.* (*Guatemala, Mexico*) prostitute.

del rejuego *exp.* (*Guatemala, Mexico*) prostitute.

> **NOTE:** This is a variation of: *del rejue.*

delantera *f.* breasts • (lit.): front part.

denso/a *n. & adj.* (*Argentina*) pain-in-the-neck; annoying • (lit.): dense.

desbeber *v.* to urinate • (lit.): to "un-drink."

desocupar *v.* to defecate • (lit.): to empty.

diablito *m.* penis, "dick" • (lit.): little devil.

diligencia (hacer una) *exp.* to go to the bathroom (urinate or defecate) • (lit.): to do an errand.

discreto/a como pedo de monja *exp.* to be indiscreet • (lit.): as discrete as a nun's fart.!

Don Juan (ser un) *m.* to be a womanizer • (lit.): to be a Don Juan (a fictitious character known for being a womanizer).

Don mierda (ser un) *exp.* to be a real nobody • (lit.): to be a Mr. Shit.

dona *f.* vagina, "pussy" • (lit.): doughnut.

dormilón/ona *n. & adj.* lazy bum; lazy • (lit.): one who sleeps a lot (from the verb *dormir* meaning "to sleep").

echar los perros *exp.* to flirt • (lit.): to throw dogs.

echar un erupto *exp.* to burp • (lit.): to throw an eruption.

el coño de la Bernarda *exp.* a real mess • (lit.): Bernarda's cunt.

> **MEXICO:** **el buey de la Bernarda** *exp.*

¡El coño de tu madre! *interj.* (*Cuba*) Fuck your mother! • (lit.): The cunt of your mother!

> **MEXICO:** **¡El carajo de tu madre!** *interj.*

el de atras *exp.* (*Mexico*) asshole • (lit.): the thing from the bottom.

el sin mangas *exp.* (*Mexico*) condom • (lit.): the one without sleeves.

elbi *m.* (*Puerto Rico*) penis, "dick."

elefante *m. & adj.* fatso; fat • (lit.): elephant.

NOTE: Although this is a masculine noun, it can be applied to a woman as well.

elote *m.* penis, "dick" • (lit.): corn on the cob.

embarazada *f.* • (lit.): pregnant.

empalmado (estar) *adj.* to get an erection • (lit.): to be connected.

empalmarse *v.* to get an erection • (lit.): to connect, to join.

empapado/a *adj.* moist • (lit.): soaking wet.

empollón/ona *n. & adj.* lazy bum; lazy • (lit.): grind.

enamoradísimo/a (estar) *adj.* to be very much in love • (lit.): to be super enamored.

enano/a *n. & adj.* runt; runty. • (lit.): dwarf.

encalomar *v.* to fornicate • (lit.): to become overheated.

encular *v.* to fornicate doggie-style, to butt-fuck • (lit.): to enter the *culo* meaning "ass."

enfermo mental (ser un) *exp.* to be crazy • (lit.): to be a mentally corrupt person.

enfermo sexual (ser un) *m.* to be a sex pervert • (lit.): to be a sexually corrupt person.

engazado/a *adj.* to be drunk • (lit.): gassed up.

enjaretarse a *v.* to fornicate • (lit.): to do (something) in a rush.

enredador/a *n. (Spain)* a gossip • (lit.): meddler.

enredoso/a *n. & adj. (Chile, Mexico)* a gossip; gossipy • (lit.): fraught with difficulties.

enrucado (estar) *adj.* to get an erection.

entabicar *v.* to fornicate • (lit.): to board up, to wall up.

entrar por detrás *exp.* to fornicate doggie-style • (lit.): to enter from the rear.

escupir *v.* to spit • (lit.): to spit.

estafiate *m. (El Savador)* asshole.

¡Esto es cagarse! *exp.* This is a fine mess! • (lit.): This is to shit oneself!

¡Esto es una cagada! *exp.* This is a fine mess! • (lit.): This is a shit!

estorbo *m.* pain-in-the-neck • (lit.): obstacle.

explorador *m.* penis, "dick" • (lit.): the explorer.

expulsar *v.* to ejaculate • (lit.): to expel, eject.

fácil *adj.* to be sexually easy • (lit.): easy.

fachar *v. (Venezuela)* to fuck a woman.

facilito/a *n. & adj.* easy lay; easy • (lit.): a little easy one.

falo *m.* penis • (lit.): phallus, penis.

faltar un tornillo *exp.* to be crazy, to have a screw loose • (lit.): to be missing a screw.

farandulero/a *n. & adj.* a gossip; gossipy • (lit.): actor, strolling player.

farolero/a (ser un/a) *n. & adj.* showoff; showy • (lit.): lantern maker.

fierro *m.* *(Mexico)* penis, "dick" • (lit.): iron.

finquita *f.* *(Puerto Rico)* vagina, "pussy" • (lit.): small piece of property.

flaco/a de mierda *n.* *(Argentina)* skinny person • (lit.): thin one of shit.

flojo/a *n. & adj.* lazy bum; lazy • (lit.): loose, weak.

foca *f.* *(Spain)* fatso • (lit.): seal.

follón *m.* • **1.** silent fart, an SBD ("silent but deadly") • **2.** jam, mess.

follón/ona *n. & adj.* lazy bum; lazy.

follar *v.* • **1.** to fart silently • **2.** to have sex.

NOTE: follón *m.* a silent fart, an SBD ("silent but deadly").

VARIATION -1: follarse *v.*

VARIATION -2: follonarse *v.*

follonarse *v.* to fart silently.
example:
Después de comerme toda esa comida picante, creo que voy a **follonarme**.

translation:
After eating all that spicy food, I think I'm going **to fart**.
NOTE: This is a variation of the term **follar**.

fondo de la espalda *m.* buttocks • (lit.): lower back.

foquin *adj.* *(Puerto Rico)* fucking.
NOTE: This is a Puerto Rican adaptation of the English adjective "fucking."

forro *m.* condom • (lit.): lining, covering.

fregón/ona *n. & adj.* pain-in-the-neck; annoying • (lit.): one who scrubs.
NOTE: This term is also commonly used to describe someone who is extremely impressive and "cool."

fregado/a *n. & adj.* annoying person, pain-in-the-neck; annoying • (lit.): scrubbing.

fresco *m.* homosexual, "fag" • (lit.): fresh.

fufú *m. & adj.* snob; stuck up • (lit.): Cuban dish made of plantain & pork rind.

fufurufu *n. & adj.* snob; stuck up.

fulana *f.* prostitute • (lit.): so-and-so (anyone).

funda *f.* condom • (lit.): lining, covering.

fundillero *m.* pimp.

fundillo *m.* anus, asshole.

NOTE: This is a variation of the masculine noun *fondillos* meaning "seat of trousers."

furcia *f.* prostitute • (lit.): doll, chick.

gafitas *m. (Spain)* lazy bum • (lit.): small eyeglasses.

galleta *f. (Costa Rica)* penis, "dick" • (lit.): cracker, cookie.

gancho *m.* pimp • (lit.): hook.

gandul/a *n. & adj.* lazy bum; lazy.

garraleta *f.* cheap whore.

garrote *m.* penis, "dick" • (lit.): club or stick.

gata *f.* vagina, "pussy" • (lit.): female cat.

gay *adj.* homosexual, gay • (lit.): [same].

gilipollas *m. (Spain)* idiot, jerk • (lit.): stupid dick.

globo *m.* condom • (lit.): balloon.

golfa *f.* prostitute • (lit.): prostitute.

goma *f.* condom • (lit.): rubber.

gomita *f.* condom • (lit.): small rubber.

gordinflón/ona *n. & adj.* fatso; fat.
NOTE: This is from the adjective *gordo* meaning "fat."

gordo/a chancho *n. & adj.* *(Argentina)* fatso; fat • (lit.): fat hog-like person.

gordo/a como una ballena *exp.* to be very fat • (lit.): as fat as a whale an elephant.
VARIATION: **gordo/a como un elefante** *adj.* • (lit.): fat as an elephant.

gordo/a de mierda *n.* *(Argentina)* fatso • (lit.): fat one of shit.

gorro *m.* condom • (lit.): cap, bonnet.

gorrona *f.* prostitute • (lit.): libertine.

gozar *v.* to ejaculate • (lit.): to enjoy.

grandote boludo *m.* *(Argentina)* big lazy bum • (lit.): big-balled (testicles) one.

grieta *f.* vagina, "pussy" • (lit.): crack.

grifear *v. (Mexico)* to smoke marijuana.

grifo *m. (Mexico)* drug addict • (lit.): faucet, tap.

grilla *f. (Mexico, Central and South America)* marijuana • (lit.): female cricket.

gritón/ona *n. & adj.* loudmouth; gossipy.
NOTE: This is from the verb *gritar* meaning "to shout."

guabina *f. (Cuba)* idiot.

guaje *m. & adj. (El Salvador, Mexico)* idiot; stupid.

example:
¿Has visto el sombrero que lleva Pancho? Le hace parecer **guaje**.

translation:
Did you see the hat Pancho is wearing? It makes him look like a **jerk**.

guante *m.* condom • (lit.): glove.

guerrillera *f. (Puerto Rico)* prostitute, whore • (lit.): guerrilla, partisan.

guey *m. & adj.* jerk, idiot; jerky • (lit.): variation of *buey* meaning "ox" or "bullock."

gumersinda *f.* heroin or opium.

gustar los bebes *exp.* to rob the cradle • (lit.): to like babies.

example:
Roberto siempre sale con mujeres mucho más jóvenes que él. Yo creo que le **gustan los bebes**.

translation:
Roberto always dates women much younger than he is. I think he likes **to rob the cradle**.

hablador/a *n. & adj.* blabbermouth; gossipy.

example:
¿Le contaste a Jesús mi secreto? ¡Qué **hablador**!

translation:
You told Jesús my secret? What a **blabbermouth**!

NOTE: This is from the verb *hablar* meaning "to speak."

hacer la barba *exp.* to brown-nose • (lit.): to do the beard.

example:
La razón por la que Ricardo ha conseguido un ascenso es porque siempre está **haciendo la barba**.

translation:
The reason Ricardo got a promotion is because he's such a **brown-noser**.

hacer la pelotilla *exp.* to brown-nose • (lit.): to do the testicle or "lick someone's balls" (since *pelotilla*, literally meaning "small balls," is used in Spanish slang to mean "small testicles").

example:
David ha debido **hacer la pelotilla** para conseguir que le subieran el sueldo.

translation:
David must have **brown-nosed** to get a raise.

hacer la sopa *exp.* to perform oral sex to a woman • (lit.): to make a soup.

hacer pipí *exp.* to urinate • (lit.): to make pee-pee.

example:
No te olvides de **hacer pipí** antes de irte a la cama.

translation:
Don't forget **to go pee-pee** before you go to bed.

hacer un cuadro *exp.* *(Cuba)* to make a daisy chain • (lit.): to make a picture.

hacer un favor *exp.* to fornicate • (lit.): to do a favor.

hacer una cubana *exp.* *(Spain)* (said of a man) to reach orgasm by rubbing the penis between a woman's breasts • (lit.): to do it Cuban-style

hacer una paja *exp.* to masturbate (someone else) / hacerse una paja *exp.* to masturbate oneself • (lit.): to make a straw.

hacerse las puñetas *exp.* to masturbate • (lit.): to make oneself cuffs.

hacerse un pajote *exp.* to masturbate • (lit.): to make a large straw.

hacerse un solitario *exp.* to masturbate • (lit.): to do a solitary.

hacerse una bartola *exp.* to masturbate • (lit.): to do a careless act.

hacerse una canuta *exp.* to masturbate • (lit.): to make a tubular container.

hacerse una carlota *exp.* to masturbate • (lit.): to do a Carlota *(a woman's name).*

hacerse una chaqueta *exp.* *(Mexico)* to masturbate • (lit.): to make a jacket.

hacerse una gallarda *exp.* to masturbate • (lit.): to make a galliard (a type of French dance).

hacerse una magnolia *exp.* to masturbate • (lit.): to make a magnolia.

hacerse una paja *exp.* to masturbate • (lit.): to make a straw.

hacerse una pera *exp.* to masturbate • (lit.): to make a pear.

hacerse una sombrillita *exp.* to masturbate • (lit.): to make a little umbrella.

¡Hay que joderse! *exp.* To hell with everything! • (lit.): One should fuck oneself!

hecho polvo *exp.* *(Spain)* said of a jerk • (lit.): made of dust.
NOTE: In Mexico, this expression is used to mean "to ache." For example: *Mis pies están hechos polvo;* My feet are aching.

hediondito *m.* vagina, "pussy" • (lit.): the little smelly one.

hermano pequeño *m.* penis, "dick" • (lit.): little brother.

hierba *f.* *(Mexico)* marijuana • (lit.): grass or herb.
NOTE: Also spelled: *yerba.*

hierro *m.* *(Puerto Rico)* penis, "dick" • (lit.): iron.

higo *m.* vagina, "pussy" • (lit.): fig (fruit).

¡Hijo de su chingada madre!
exp. You son of a bitch! • (lit.): Son of your fucked mother!

¡Hijo de tu chingada madre!
interj. You son of a bitch! • (lit.): Son of your fucking mother!
example:
¡Me has estropeado mi bicicleta nueva! **¡Hijo de tu chingada madre**!
translation:
You ruined my new bicycle! **You son of a bitch**!

hinchapelotas *m.*
pain-in-the-neck • (lit.): one who makes someone's testicles swell.
example:
No puedo aguantar a Marco. Es un **hinchapelotas**. ¡Usa mis cosas sin pedírmelas!
translation:
I can't stand Marco. He's a **pain-in-the-neck**. He borrows my things without asking!
NOTE: pelotas *f.pl.* testicles • (lit.): balls (in a game).

hocicón/ona *n. & adj.* loudmouth; gossipy • (lit.): mouthy (since this term comes from the masculine noun *hocico* meaning "snout").
example:
No quiero invitar a Anita a mi fiesta porque no la soporto. ¡Es tan **hocicona**!
translation:
I don't want to invite Anita to my party because I can't stand her. She's such a **loudmouth**!

hocicar *v.* to fornicate • (lit.): to root, nuzzle, grub around in.

holgazán/ana *n. & adj.* lazy bum; lazy • (lit.): lazy, indolent.
example:
Odio esta camisa. Me hace parecer un **holgazán**.
translation:
I hate this shirt. It makes me look like a **geek**.

¡Hostia puta! *interj.* Holy shit! • (lit.): Fucking sacred wafer!
example:
¡Hostia puta! ¡Mira cómo llueve!
translation:
Holy Shit! Look at all that rain!

hoyo *m. (Puerto Rico)* vagina, "pussy" • (lit.): hole.

hueso *m.* penis, "dick" • (lit.): bone.

huevón/ona (ser un) *n. & adj.* lazy bum; lazy • (lit.): to be like a testicle (since *huevón* comes from the term *huevo* which literally means "egg" but it used in slang to mean "testicle").
example:
Mi hermano y yo somos completamente opuestos. Yo soy muy activo y él es un **huevón**.
translation:
My brother and I are totally opposite. I'm very motivated and he's a **lazy bum**.

huevos *m.pl.* testicles • (lit.): eggs.
NOTE -1: In Bolivia, this term means "homosexual," or closer, "faggot."

NOTE -2: **costar un huevo** *exp.* to be terribly expensive, "to cost one's left nut" • (lit.): to cost one testicle.

NOTE -3: **huevada** *f.* stupidity.

NOTE -4: **huevón** *adj.* a description of a lazy or stupid person • (lit.): one with big *huevos* or "balls."

NOTE -5: **tener huevos** *exp.* to be courageous • (lit.): to have balls.

I

impermeable *m.* (*Mexico*) condom • (lit.): raincoat.

inga *f.* (*Cuba*) penis, "dick" • (lit.): inga plant.

insinuarse a alguien *exp.* to lead someone on • (lit.): to hint oneself to someone.

example:
Tienes que dejar de **insinuarte a él** y ser honesta con tus sentimientos.

translation:
You need to **stop leading him on** and be honest about your feelings.

inspector de zócalo *m.* (*Argentina*) runt • (lit.): baseboard inspector.

example:
¿Le pediste a Enrique que te ayudara a mover el piano? ¡Pero si es un **inspector de zócalo**!

translation:
You asked Enrique to help you move your piano? But he's such a **little runt**!

instrumento *m.* penis, "dick" • (lit.): instrument.

invertido *adj.* homosexual, "fag" • (lit.): inverted.

ir a botar el agua al canario *exp.* (*Cuba*) to go take a leak • (lit.): to go to throw away the canary's water.

example:
Creo que he bebido demasiado café; necesito **ir a botar el agua al canario** otra vez.

translation:
I think I drank too much coffee. I need **to take a leak** again.

ir a desgastar el petate *exp.* (*Mexico*) to have sex • (lit.): to go wear down the bedding.

ir a desvencigar la cama *exp.* (*Mexico*) to have sex • (lit.): to go break the bed.

ir a hacer de las aguas *exp.* (*Mexico*) to have sex • (lit.): to go make some water.

ir a la junta de consiliación *exp.* (*Mexico*) to have sex • (lit.): to go to a meeting.

ir a la lucha super libre a calzón *exp.* (*Mexico*) to have sex • (lit.): to go see wrestling wearing nothing but underwear.

ir a percudir el cochón *exp.* (*Mexico*) to have sex • (lit.): to tarnish the mattress.

ir a rechinar la cama *exp.* (*Mexico*) to have sex • (lit.): to make the bed squeak.

ir a un entierro *exp.* (*Mexico*) to have sex • (lit.): to go to a funeral.

ir con el culo a rastras *exp.* • **1.** to be in a jam • **2.** to be broke • (lit.): to go with the ass dragging.

ir de culo *exp.* to go downhill, to deteriorate • (lit.): to go on its ass.

irse *v.* to ejaculate • (lit.): to leave, go away.

irse a la gloria *exp.* to ejaculate • (lit.): to go to the glory.

irse de la varilla *exp.* to ejaculate • (lit.): to go from the stick.

J

¡Jódete y aprieta el culo! *exp.* (*Cuba*) Go fuck yourself! • (lit.): Fuck you and hold your ass tight!
example:
¡Me has engañado! **¡Jódete y aprieta el culo!**
translation:
You cheated me! **Go fuck yourself!**

jaina *f.* prostitute.

jamón/ona *n. & adj.* fatso; fat • (lit.): ham.
example:
¡Vaya **jamona**! ¡Debe pesar una tonelada!

translation:
What a **fatso**! She must weigh a ton!

jardinera *f.* homosexual, "fag" • (lit.): female gardener.

jeba *f.* (*Puerto Rico*) prostitute, whore.
NOTE: This is a variation of the masculine noun *jebe* meaning "alum."

jebo *m.* (*Puerto Rico*) pimp.

jiñar *v.* • **1.** to urinate • **2.** to defecate.
example:
¡Tengo que encontrar un sitio donde **jiñar**!
translation:
I need to find somewhere **to relieve myself**!

joda *f.* • **1.** nuisance • *Esto es una joda;* This is a nuisance • **2.** joke • *Alfonso me dijo una buena joda;* Alfonso told me a good joke.

joder *v.* • **1.** to fuck • **2.** to annoy • **3.** to steal • **4.** to fuck up • **5.** failure, flop • **6.** *interj.* Fuck! (used to denote anger, surprise, disappointment) • *¡Joder! ¡Dejame en paz!;* Fuck! Leave me alone!

joder como desesperados *exp.* to fornicate • (lit.): to fuck like desperate people.

joder como locos *exp.* to fornicate • (lit.): to fuck like crazy people.

joderse *v.* to be annoying • *Esto me jode;* This is annoying me.

joderse vivos *exp.* to fornicate • (lit.): to fuck alive.

jodida/pinche puta *f.* fucking bitch • (lit.): fucking whore.
underline: example:
¡Ésa **jodida/pinche puta** me ha zancadilleado!
underline: translation:
That **fucking bitch** tripped me!
NOTE: In Spain, the adjective *jodida* would be used in this expression, whereas in Mexico, the commonly used adjective would be *pinche.*

jodido/a *adj.* • **1.** exhausted, wiped out • *Después de trabajar todo el fin de semana, estoy jodido;* After working all weekend I'm wiped out. • **2.** difficult • *Yo creo que el examen era muy jodido;* I think the test was very difficult. • **3.** fucking • *¡Guillermo es un jodido idiota!;* Guillermo is such a fucking idiot! • **4.** ruined • *¡Derramé jugo de tomate en mi chaleco nuevo y lo jodí!;* I spilled tomato juice on my new sweater and ruined it! • **5.** destitute, broke • *Clarissa perdió un montón de dinero en las apuestas; Ahora está jodida;* Clarissa lost all of her money gambling. Now she's broke. • (lit.): fucked.

jodido/a pero contento/a *exp.* a common response to someone asking how you're doing • (lit.): fucked but content.

jodienda *f.* annoying person or thing, pain-in-the-ass • (lit.): act of fucking.

jodón/ona *n. & adj.* pain-in-the-ass; fucking annoying.

jodontón/ona *n. & adj.* "horndog"; sexual, horny.

josiadora *f. (Puerto Rico)* prostitute, whore.

joto *m. (Mexico)* homosexual, "fag" • (lit.): effeminate.

jugo *m.* semen • (lit.): juice.

¡La concha de tu madre! *interj. (Uruguay)* an extremely vulgar insult literally meaning "Your mother's cunt!"
VARIATION: El concho de tu madre! *interj.*

¡La puta que te parió! *interj.* You son of a bitch! • (lit.): The whore that gave you birth!
underline: example:
¿Cómo has podido hacer algo tan horrible? ¡**La puta que te parió**!
underline: translation:
How could you do such a horrible thing? **You son of a bitch**!

lacho *m. (Puerto Rico)* vagina, "pussy."

lagarta f. • **1.** prostitute, whore • **2.** bitch • (lit.): lizard.

lagartona f. • **1.** prostitute, whore • **2.** bitch • (lit.): big lizard.
example:
Karen se acuesta con todos. ¡Estoy empezando a pensar que es una **lagarta**!
translation:
Karen has sex with everybody. I am starting to think she's a **whore**!

lambiscón/ona n. & adj.
brown-noser.
example:
Eduardo Haskell es muy cumplido con mi madre; es un **lambiscón**.
translation:
Eduardo Haskell always gives my mother compliments. He's such a **brown-noser**

lameculo[s] m. & adj. kiss-ass, brown-noser • (lit.): butt-licker.
example:
¿Has oido cómo le hablaba Ana al jefe? Nunca supe que fuera tan **lameculo[s]**.
translation:
Did you hear how Ana was talking to the boss? I never knew she was such a **kiss-ass**.

lamehuevos m. brown-noser • (lit.): egg (testicles) sucker.
example:
¡Ese **lamehuevos** acaba de ser ascendido!
translation:
That **brown-noser** just got a promotion!

lamepollas m. cocksucker • (lit.): [same].

example:
El primo de Pablo es un **lamepollas**. ¡No lo soporto!
translation:
Pablo's cousin is a **cocksucker**. I can't stand him!

lamer el culo de alguien exp. to kiss up to someone • (lit.): to lick someone's ass.

lamesuelas m. & adj. kiss-ass • (lit.): leather licker.
example:
La razón por la que al jefe le gusta tanto Victor es porque éste es un **lamesuelas**.
translation:
The reason the boss likes Victor so much is because he's such a **kiss-ass**.

lanzar v. to ejaculate • (lit.): to throw.

largo al pedo m. (Argentina) tall man • (lit.): long or tall fart.
example:
¡Qué **largo al pedo**! Debe ser jugador de baloncesto.
translation:
What a **tall man**! He must be a basketball player.
VARIATION: **lungo al pedo** m.

latoso/a n. & adj.
pain-in-the-neck; annoying person • (lit.): made of tin can.
example:
Diana es una **latosa**. No hace más que pedirme favores.

translation:
Diana is a **pain-in-the-neck**. All she ever does is ask me for favors.

leche f. semen • (lit.): milk.

NOTE: This term may also be used as an expletive.

ALSO -1: **de mala leche** adj. said of someone who is mean • (lit.): of bad semen.

ALSO -2: **hay mucha mala leche entre ellos** exp. there are a lot of bad feelings between them • (lit.): there's a lot of bad semen between them.

ALSO -3: **tener mala leche** exp. to be in a bad mood • (lit.): to have bad semen.

lechero m. penis, "dick."

NOTE: This is from leche literally meaning "milk" but used in slang to mean "semen."

lengua larga (tener) exp. (Argentina) to be a blabbermouth • (lit.): to have a long tongue.
example:
A Angel le encanta chismear de la gente. **Tiene la lengua larga**.
translation:
Angel loves to gossip about people. **He's a blabbermouth**.

lenguasuelta n. & adj. (Mexico) a gossip; gossipy • (lit.): loose tongue.
example:
¡Para de ser **lenguasuelta**! No son mas que mentiras.
translation:
Stop being a **gossip**! Those are nothing but lies.

lenguatuda f. (Argentina) blabbermouth • (lit.): one with a long tongue (used for blabbing).
example:
Consuela no puede guardar un secreto. Es una **lenguatuda**.
translation:
Consuela can't keep a secret. She's such a **blabbermouth**.

leña f. (Cuba) penis, "dick" • (lit.): firewood.

licor m. semen • (lit.): liquor.

limones m.pl. breasts • (lit.): lemons.

limpiar el sable exp. to fornicate • (lit.): to clean the saber.

lina f. (Mexico) line of cocaine • (lit.): line.

llello m. (Mexico, Puerto Rico) cocaine, crack.

lleno/a de humos adj. (Argentina) snobby • (lit.): full of smoke.
example:
La tía de David está **llena de humos**. Se niega a hablar con la gente que no es rica.
translation:
David's aunt is **very snobby**. She refuses to speak to people who aren't rich.

loca *m.* *(Venezuela)* homosexual, "fag," transvestite • (lit.): crazy woman.

loco/a como una cabra (estar) *exp.* to be crazy • (lit.): to be as crazy as a nanny goat.
example:
Si yo fuera tú no confiaría en él. ¡Está **loco como una cabra**!
translation:
I wouldn't trust him if I were you. He's **out of his mind**!

loco/a de remate (estar) *exp.* to be crazy • (lit.): to be crazy to the end.
example:
Si piensas que voy a salir con Manuel, ¡es que estás **loco de remate**!
translation:
If you think I'm going to go out with Manuel, you're **nuts**!

locote *n.* big idiot.
example:
Mi hermana es psiquiatra y trabaja con **locotes** todo el día.
translation:
My sister is a psychiatrist who works with **crazy people** all day long.
NOTE: This comes from the adjective *loco/a* meaning "crazy."

longaniza *f.* penis, "dick" • (lit.): pork sausage.

lungo de mierda *m.* *(Argentina)* very tall person • (lit.): long or tall shit.

lurio/a *adj.* *(Mexico)* crazy • (lit.): mad, crazy.
example:
Si te crees que te puedes comer esa tarta entera, tú estás **lurio**.
translation:
If you think you can eat that entire cake, you're **crazy**.
VARIATION: **lurias** *adj.*

luz de mierda *f.* *(Argentina)* smart person • (lit.): light of shit.

ménage à trois *m.* threesome • (lit.): house of three people.

¡Métetelo por el culo! *exp.* Shove it up your ass! • (lit.): Put it in your ass!

macana *f.* penis, "dick" • (lit.): heavy wooden club.

macha *f. & adj.* lesbian • (lit.): the feminine form of *macho* meaning "very masculine."

machaca *f.* penis, "dick" • (lit.): crusher, pounder.

machete *m.* penis, "dick" • (lit.): machete.

machorra *f.* lesbian.
NOTE: This is a variation of the masculine noun *macho* meaning "manly."

madama *f.* *(Mexico)* madame of a brothel.

madre f. (Mexico) mother fucker • (lit.): mother.

ALSO: **me vale madre** exp. I don't give a fuck • (lit.): it's worth a mother to me.

madre superiora f. (Mexico) a madame of a brothel • (lit.): mother superior.

madrina f. (Mexico) a madame of a brothel • (lit.): godmother.

madrota f. (Mexico) a madame of a brothel.

NOTE: This is a variation of the feminine noun madrona meaning "pampering mother."

magras f.pl. buttocks • (lit.): slice of ham, rasher.

maja f. elegant woman.
example:
¿Has visto a Sandra? ¡Ella es muy **maja**!
translation:
Have you see Sandra? She's a really **elegant woman**!

maje adj. crazy.
example:
Tú estás **maje** si crees que el jefe te va a conceder un ascenso.
translation:
You're **out of your mind** if you think the boss is going to give you a raise.
NOTE: This is from the verb majar meaning "to crush, pound, mash."

majo m classy guy.
example:
¿Crees que David es un **majo**?

translation:
Do you believe that David is a **classy guy**?

mal aire m. fart • (lit.): bad air.
example:
¡Qué asco! ¡Creo que huelo un **mal aire**!
translation:
Yuck! I think I smell a **fart**!

mala semana f. menstruation • (lit.): bad week.

maldita puta f. damned bitch • (lit.): damned whore.
example:
¡Esa **maldita puta** ha derramado jugo de tomate en mi chaleco nuevo!
translation:
That **bitch** spilled tomato juice on my new sweater!

maleta f. prostitute, whore • (lit.): suitcase.

malva f. (Mexico) marijuana • (lit.): mallow.

mamada f. blow job • (lit.): sucking.

mamón/ona n. & adj. •
1. brown-noser • **2.** obnoxious person.
example:
Rolando le ha comprado el almuerzo al jefe por tercera vez en esta semana. ¡Qué **mamón**!
translation:
Rolando bought the boss lunch for the third time this week. What a **brown-noser**!
NOTE: This is from the verb mamar meaning "to suck."

mamplora f. (El Salvador) homosexual, "fag."

manchas f.pl. breasts, "tits" • (lit.): spots or stains.

mandarria f. (Cuba) penis, "dick" • (lit.): sledge hammer.

manga f. (Mexico) condom • (lit.): sleeve.

mango m. sexy person, hot number • (lit.): mango.
example:
¡Mi maestra de biología es un **mango**!
translation:
My biology teacher is a **hot number**!

manguera f. penis, "dick" • (lit.): water hose.

manitas (hacer) exp.
example:
No pienso volver a salir con Eric. ¡Empezó a **hacer manitas** conmigo en el restaurante!
translation:
I'm never going out with Eric again. He started **playing footsie** with me at the restaurant!
NOTE: This is from the feminine noun mano meaning "hand" or "paw."

manolo m. penis, "dick."
NOTE: This is a variation of the name Manuel.

manosear v. to finger [someone] • (lit.): to touch with one's hands.

manudo/a n. (El Salvador) drunkard.

example:
No pienso volver a invitar al **manudo** de Rafael a mi casa nunca más. ¡Fue tan vergonzoso!
translation:
I'm never inviting that **drunkard** Rafael to my house again. He was so embarrassing!

marchatrás m. (Argentina) homosexual, "fag" • (lit.): one who goes backward.

margaritas f.pl. breasts, "tits" • (lit.): pearls.

marica m. homosexual, "fag" • (lit.): magpie.

maricón m. **1.** anus • **2.** homosexual, "fag" • (lit.): sissy, homosexual, queer.

maricona f. homosexual, "fag" • (lit.): homosexual.

marimacha f. lesbian, "dyke."
NOTE: This is a variation of the feminine noun marica meaning "sissy" and the adjective macho meaning "manly."

mariposa f. (Mexico) homosexual, "fag" • (lit.): butterfly.

mariquita f. homosexual male, "fag" • (lit.): ladybird.

mariscala f. (Mexico) a madame of a brothel.

mary f. (Mexico) marijuana.

mastuerzo m. (Mexico) marijuana.

mazo m. penis, "dick" • (lit.): mallet.

¡Me cago en el recontracoño de tu reputísima madre! exp. (Cuba – extremely vulgar) Fuck you! • (lit.): I shit on the super cunt of your super whore mother!

¡Me cago en la madre que te parió! exp. Fuck you! • (lit.): I shit in the mother who gave you birth!

¡Me cago en la mar! exp. (Spain) Fuck that shit! • (lit.): I shit in the ocean!

¡Me cago en la purimísima hostia! exp. Fuck it all! • (lit.): I shit on the holiest communion wafer!

¡Me cago en tí! exp. Fuck you! • (lit.): I shit on you!

¡Me cago en tu madre! exp. Fuck you! • (lit.): I shit on your mother!
example:
¡Cómo eres capaz de hacerme eso! **¡Me cago en tu madre**!

translation:
How dare you do such a mean thing to me! **Fuck you**!

VARIATION: **¡Me cago en el recontracoño de tu reputísima madre!** exp. (Cuba – extremely vulgar) • (lit.): I shit on the super cunt of your super whore mother!

¡Me cago en tus huesos! exp. Fuck you! • (lit.): I shit in your bones!

¡Me cago en tus mulas! exp. Fuck you! • (lit.): I shit in your mules!

meón n. baby, "little pisher" (from the verb mear meaning "to piss").
example:
¿Has visto a ese **meón**? ¡Es tan lindo!

translation:
Did you see that **little kid**? He's so cute!

meadero m. urinal (from the verb mear meaning "to piss").
example:
El **meadero** en este baño está tan limpio.

translation:
The **urinal** in this bathroom is so clean.

meado[s] m.pl. urine, piss (from the verb mear meaning "to piss").
example:
El olor a **meado** me pone enfermo.

translation:
The smell of **urine** makes me sick.

mear v. to urinate, to piss.
example:
Creo que tengo que llevar a mi hija al baño. Parece que necesita **mear**.

translation:
I think I need to take my daughter to the bathroom. She looks like she need **to take a leak**.

NOTE: **mearse de risa** exp. to laugh so hard as to urinate in one's pants • (lit.): [same].

mecasala f. (El Salvador) penis, "dick."

melocotones m.pl. breasts, "tits" • (lit.): peaches.

melones m.pl. breasts, "tits" • (lit.): melons.

mendigo/a n. & adj. tightwad; stingy • (lit.): beggar, mendicant.
example:
¿Te puedes creer el regalo tan barato que me hizo Geraldo para mi cumpleaños? ¡Qué **mendigo**!
translation:
Can you believe the cheap gift Geraldo gave me for my birthday? What a **cheapskate**!

meneársela v. to masturbate, to beat off • (lit.): to shake it for oneself.

menso/a (Mexico) n. & adj. idiot; jerky • (lit.): foolish, stupid.
example:
Acabo de enterarme de que Carla está en un hospital psiquiátrico. No sabía que estaba **mensa**.
translation:
I just heard that Carla is in a mental hospital. I didn't know she was **nuts**.

merengue f. (Spain) beautiful woman • (lit.): meringue (since meringue is so sweet).
example:
¿Ves a ese **merengue** allí? ¡Creo que te está mirando!
translation:
See that **hot chick** over there? I think she's looking at you!

mermelada de membrillo f. (Mexico) semen • (lit.): marmalade of the smaller limb.

mesero sin charola m. homosexual male, "fag" • (lit.): waiter without a tray (since the hand is in an effeminate position with the palm facing upward).

meter el dedo exp. to finger [someone] • (lit.): to put the finger.

meterla de mira quien viene exp. (Cuba) to fornicate doggie-style, to fornicate through the anus • (lit.): to put it in looking to see who is coming.
VARIATION: **singar de mira quien viene** exp.

meterla hasta la empuñadura exp. to fornicate • (lit.): to put in up to the sword hilt.

meterla hasta las cachas exp. to fornicate • (lit.): to put it up to the buttocks.

meterla hasta los huevos exp. to fornicate • (lit.): to put it up to the balls (testicles).

meterla hasta los puños exp. to fornicate • (lit.): to put it up to the fists.

metersela a alguien exp. to fornicate • (lit.): to put it in someone.

mico/a n. (Central America) vagina, "pussy" • (lit.): car jack.

miembrillo m. (Mexico) penis, "dick" • (lit.): small member.

mierda • **1.** *interj.* shit (used to express surprise, anger, disappointment) • **2.** filth • (lit.): shit.

mierda (ser una) *exp.* said of a despicable person • (lit.): to be a shit.

mierdecilla *f.* runt • (lit.) little shit.
example:
Ese **mierdecilla** es un presuntuoso y ni siquiera le gusta a nadie.
translation:
That **little runt** acts so conceited but no one even likes him.

mierdero *m.* (*Nicaragua*) scum • (lit.): a place where there is a lot of shit.

mierdita *f.* a worthless piece of shit • (lit.): little shit.

minga *f.* penis, "dick" • (lit.): communal work.

minina *f.* (*child's language*) penis, "pee-pee" • (lit.): kitty cat.

minino *m.* (*child's language*) vagina • (lit.): kitty cat.

mirasol *m.* penis, "dick" • (lit.): sunflower.

mitotero/a *n. & adj.* a gossip; gossipy • (lit.): rowdy, noisy person.
example:
Te lo advierto, Margarita es una verdadera **mitotera**. No le cuentes nada personal.
translation:
I'm warning you. Margarita is a real **gossip**. Don't tell her anything personal.

mitra *f.* (*Puerto Rico*) penis, "dick" • (lit.): mitre.

mocongó *m.* (*Puerto Rico*) penis, "dick."

mocoso/a de mierda *n.* (*Argentina*) snot-nosed little brat • (lit.): snotty one of shit.

mojado/a *adj.* moist • (lit.): wet.

mojar [el churro] *exp.* to fornicate • (lit.): to wet [the long fritter].
NOTE: **churro** *m.* a long, straight fried pastry.

molesto/a como mosca de letrina *exp.* annoying • (lit.): annoying as an outhouse fly.
example:
¡Vete! ¡Eres **molesto como una mosca de letrina**!
translation:
Go away! You're **so annoying**!

mona *f.* (*El Salvador*) penis, "dick" • (lit.): female monkey.

montar *v.* to fornicate • (lit.): to climb up (on someone).

moravia *f.* (*Mexico*) marijuana.

morcilla *f.* penis, "dick" • (lit.): blood sausage.

morder *v.* to give a French kiss • (lit.): to bite.

morisqueta *f.* (*Mexico*) marijuana • (lit.): speck.

morreo *m.* French kiss.
NOTE: This is a variation of the masculine noun *morro* meaning "snout."

morronga f. (Central America) penis, "dick" • (lit.): a female cat.

morrongo m. (Mexico) penis, "dick" • (lit.): male cat.

mota f. (Mexico) marijuana.

motivosa f. (Mexico) marijuana.
NOTE: This is a variation of the masculine noun motivo meaning "motive" or "reason."

motocicleta f. (Mexico) marijuana • (lit.): motorcycle.

motor de chorro m. (Mexico) marijuana • (lit.): jet engine.

motorizar v. (Mexico, Central and South America) to smoke marijuana • (lit.): to motorize.

muchachas putierrez f.pl. (Mexico, Guatemala) prostitutes • (lit.): Putierrez girls.
NOTE: The feminine noun putierrez is a variation of the term puta meaning prostitute and is used here in jest as the girls' last name.

muerdo m. a French kiss, a kiss with the tongue.
NOTE: This comes from the verb morder meaning "to bite."

mujer de la calle f. prostitute • (lit.): a woman of the street.

mujer de la vida galante f. prostitute • (lit.): woman of luxurious lifestyle.

mujer fatal f. prostitute • (lit.): wicked woman.

mujeriego m. & adj. skirt-chaser; obsessed with women • (lit.): one who is obsessed with women (from the feminine noun mujer meaning "woman").
example:
Nunca saldría con alguien tan **mujeriego** como Simón. No creo que él pudiera ser fiel.
translation:
I would never go out with such a **skirt-chaser** as Simón. I don't think he could ever be faithful.

muñeco m. (Mexico) vagina, "pussy" • (lit.): doll, puppet.

nabo m. penis, "dick" • (lit.): turnip.

nalgón n. a person with a big buttocks • (lit.): someone with a large buttocks.

nalga de angel f. (Mexico) marijuana • (lit.): buttocks of an angel.

nalgas f.pl. • **1.** buttocks • **2.** vagina • (lit.): buttocks.

necio/a n. & adj. fool; foolish • (lit.): foolish.
example:
La gente que no practica el sexo de forma segura es una **necia**.
translation:
People who don't practice safe sex are **crazy**.

néctar *m.* semen • (lit.): nectar.

nene *small child (Puerto Rico)* penis, "dick" • (lit.): small child.

nido *m. (Mexico)* vagina • (lit.): bird's nest or hiding place.

no importar un carajo *exp.* not to give a damn • (lit.): not to mind a penis.

example:
Jorge **no me importa un carajo**. Ya no somos amigos.

translation:
I **don't give a damn** about Jorge. We're not friends any more.

no importar un cojón *exp.* not to give a damn • (lit.): not to care a testicle.

example:
A Beatriz **no le importan un cojón** sus clases. Por eso está suspendiendolo todo.

translation:
Beatriz **doesn't give a damn** about her school work. That's why she's failing all of her classes.

no importar un huevo *exp.* not to give a damn • (lit.): egg (or "testicle").

example:
A Daniel no le importa un huevo su trabajo. Sinceramente, creo que le van a echar pronto.

translation:
Daniel doesn't give a damn about his job. Frankly, I think he's going to get fired soon.

no importar un pepino *exp.* not to give a hoot • (lit.): not to care a cucumber.

example:
No me importa un pepino lo que la gente piense de mí.

translation:
I don't give a damn what people think about me.

¡No me jodas! *exp.* Don't fuck around with me! • (lit.): Don't fuck me!

novia *f.* girlfriend • (lit.): bride, fiancée.

example:
¿Esa es tu **novia**? ¡Enhorabuena! ¡Es muy simpática y tan bonita!

translation:
That's your **girlfriend**? Congratulations! She's very nice and so beautiful!

novio *m.* boyfriend • (lit.): bridegroom, fiancé.

example:
¿Conoces a mi **novio**? Creo que nos vamos a casar algún día.

translation:
Did you meet my **boyfriend**? I think we're going to get married someday.

ñema *f. (Santo Domingo)* penis, "dick."

ALSO: **macañema** *f.* cocksucker (from the verb *mascar* meaning "to chew").

O

obraderas *f.pl.* *(Mexico)* diarrhea (from the verb *obrar* meaning "to make a bowel movement").
example:
Si bebes agua en ese país, puedes coger **obraderas**.
translation:
If you drink the water in that country, you may get **diarrhea**.

obrar *v.* to defecate • (lit.): to perform or to build.
example:
Si tu perro **obra** en la acera, tienes que limpiarlo.
translation:
If your dog **craps** on the sidewalk, you need to clean it up.

obstaculos *m.pl.* *(Mexico)* testicles • (lit.): obstacles.

ojal *m.* • vagina, "pussy" (lit.): buttonhole, slit.

ojete *m.* anal sphincter • (lit.): eyelet, eyehole.
NOTE: In Mexico, this term is also used to describe someone who is a pain-in-the-neck. For example: *Miguel es un ojete*; Miguel is a pain-in-the-neck.

ojitos (hacer) *exp.* to lead someone on • (lit.): to make little eyes.
example:
Creo que Ricardo te está **haciendo ojitos** porque ayer le ví en el cine con otra chica.

translation:
I think Ricardo is **leading you on** because yesterday I saw him at the movies with another girl.

ojo del culo *m.* anal sphincter • (lit.): eye of the ass.

orégano *m.* *(Mexico)* marijuana • (lit.): oregano.

orégano chino *m.* *(Mexico)* marijuana • (lit.): Chinese oregano.

orto *m.* *(Argentina, Uruguay)* ass • (lit.): rise of the sun or a star.

ostentador/a *n. & adj.* showoff; showy • (lit.): one who is ostentatious.
example:
¿Has visto lo que llevaba Claudia puesto? ¡Qué **ostentadora**!
translation:
Did you see what Claudia was wearing? What a **showoff**!

P

pacaya *f.* *(El Salvador)* penis, "dick" • (lit.): elongated vegetable.

padrote *m.* pimp • (lit.): large father.

pahuela *f.* prostitute, whore.

paja *f.* masturbation • (lit.): straw •*hacer una paja*; to jerk off.

pajarito *m.* penis, "dick" • (lit.): small bird.

pajero *m.* a person who masturbates.

palo *m.* penis, "dick" • (lit.): pole, stick.

> **NOTE: echar un palo** *exp.* to fornicate • (lit.): to throw the stick or "penis."

palo (echar un) *exp.* to fornicate • (lit.): to throw a stick or "penis."

> **NOTE: palo** *m.* penis, "dick" • (lit.): stick, pole.

pan *m.* (*El Salvador*) vagina • (lit.): bread.

pandero *m.* buttocks • (lit.): large tambourine.

panocha *f.* (*Mexico*) vagina, "pussy" • (lit.): sweetbread.

panuda *f.* (*El Salvador*) large vagina.

panzón/ona *n. & adj.* fat slob; chubby, fat.
example:
Cecila estaba tan delgada. Ahora es una **panzona**.
translation:
Cecilia used to be so thin. Now she's a **fat slob**.

panzudo al pedo *adj.* (*Argentina*) extremely fat • (lit.): paunchy to the fart.
example:
Mi tío es **panzudo al pedo**. ¡Le encanta comer!
translation:
My uncle is **fat out to here**. He loves to eat!

papasito *m. & adj.* a hot daddy; sexy • (lit.): little father.
example:
Carlos tiene muchas novias. Es un **papasito**!
translation:
Carlos has a lot of girfriends. He's such a **hunk**!

papaya *f.* (*Cuba, Puerto Rico, Central America*) vagina, "pussy."

> **NOTE:** In Cuba, the papaya fruit is called *fruta bomba,* or literally, "bomb fruit" (or "fruit shaped like a bomb").

papayón/ona *n. & adj.* (*Cuba*) asshole, jerk; jerky • (lit.): big vagina (since *papaya* is used to mean "vagina" in Cuba).
example:
¿Has invitado tú a esa **papayón** a la fiesta?
translation:
You invited that **asshole** to your party?

papo/a *n. & adj.* (*El Salvador*) idiot; crazy.
example:
Jaime es un **papo** si piensa que va ser médico algún día. No es lo suficientemente listo.
translation:
Jaime is a **nut** if he thinks he's going to be a doctor someday. He's not smart enough.

paracaídas *m.* condom • (lit.): parachute.

paraguas *m.* condom • (lit.): umbrella.

pararse *v.* to get an erection • (lit.): to stand up.

pargo *m.* *(Cuba)* homosexual, "fag" • (lit.): red snapper.

parlanchín *m.* blabbermouth • (lit.): talkative.
example:
Armando habla sin parar. Es un **parlanchín**.
translation:
Armando talks nonstop. He's a **blabbermouth**.

parrocha *f.* vagina, "pussy" • (lit.): small pickled sardine.

parte de atrás *m.* buttocks • (lit.): behind part.

parte posterior *m.* buttocks • (lit.): posterior part.

partes *f.pl.* genitals • (lit.): parts.

partes nobles *f.pl.* penis, "dick" • (lit.): noble parts.

pasar por la piedra *exp.* to fornicate • (lit.): to pass by the stone.

pasar por las armas *exp.* to fornicate • (lit.): to pass by the arms.

pashpa *f.* *(El Salvador)* vagina, "pussy".

pato *m.* homosexual, "fag" • (lit.): duck.

pecho *m.* chest.

pechonalidad *m.* breasts, "tits."
NOTE: This is a variation of the feminine noun *personalidad* meaning "personality."

pechos *m.pl.* breasts, "tits" • (lit.): breasts.

pedazo *m.* *(Uruguay)* penis, "dick" • (lit.): piece.

pedazo de pelotudo *m.* *(Argentina)* jerk, idiot • (lit.): piece of someone with balls.
example:
¡Le dejé mi coche a Jaime y el **pedazo de pelotudo** lo estrelló contra una pared!
translation:
I lent my car to Jaime and that **idiot** crashed it into a wall!

pederse *v.* to fart • (lit.): to fart.
example:
¡No me puedo creer que **te pedas** en mi coche!
translation:
I can't believe **you'd fart** in my car!

pedo *m.* • **1.** fart • **2.** drunkenness • **3.** ugly.
example -1:
Ese chiste es tan gracioso como un **pedo** en un traje espacial.
translation:
That joke is as funny as a **fart** in a space suit.
example -2:
Manolo agarró un buen **pedo** en la fiesta.
translation:
Manolo got really **drunk** at the party.
example -3:
Ese tipo es un **pedo**.
translation:
That guy is an **ugly person**.

pedorrera *f.* many farts, a series of farts.

example:
¿Has oído esa **pedorrera**? ¡Qué asco!

translation:
Did you hear **all that farting**? That's disgusting!

pedorrero *m.* one who farts a lot, farter.

example:
Mi tío tiene problemas de estómago. Es un **pedorrero**.

translation:
My uncle has gastric problems. He's a **farter**.

peerse *v.* to fart • (lit.): to fart

example:
Es de mala educación **peerse** en público.

translation:
It's rude **to fart** in public.

pelársela *v.* to masturbate • (lit.): to peel it oneself.

película equis *f.* dirty movie, X-rated movie • (lit.): an X(-rated) movie.

example:
¡No podemos llevar a los niños a ver eso...es una **película equis**!

translation:
We can't take the children to see that...it's an **X-rated movie**!

pelmazo/a *n.* idiot • (lit.): undigested food.

example:
¡Ese **pelmazo** se ha saltado un semáforo en rojo!

translation:
That **idiot** ran a red light!

pelón/ona *n. & adj.* baldy; bald.

example:
Enrique tiene solamente diez y seis años y él ya está **pelón**.

translation:
Enrique is only sixteen years old and he's already **bald**.

pelona *f.* penis, "dick."

NOTE: This is from the adjective *pelón* meaning "bald."

pelota *n. & adj.* **1.** kiss-ass • **2.** idiot; stupid • (lit.): ball (or one who "licks someone's balls or testicles").

example -1:
El único motivo por el que Roberto fue ascendido, es porque es un **pelota**.

translation:
The only reason Roberto got a promotion is because he's a **kiss-ass**.

ALSO: **pelota** *adj.* (Colombia) stupid.

example -2:
¡Marco es tan **pelota**! ¡El manejó en la calle en sentido contrario!

translation:
Marco is such an **idiot**! He drove down the street in the wrong direction!

pelotas *n. & adj.* (Colombia) dumbbell, idiot; stupid • (lit.): that which has with balls.

example:
¡Antonio se lavó el pelo con pasta dentrífica! ¡Qué **pelotas**!

translation:
Antonio accidentally washed his hair with toothpaste! What an **idiot**!

> **NOTE:** **tener pelotas** *exp.* to have courage • (lit.): to have balls.

pelotas michinadas *f.pl. (Mexico, Central and South America)* blue balls.

pelotudo/a *n. & adj.* idiot; stupid.
example:
Se me ha olvidado mi cita con el médico. ¡Qué **pelotudo**!
translation:
I forgot about my doctor's appointment. What an **idiot**!

> **NOTE:** This is from the feminine noun *pelota* meaning "ball."

pelotudo y boludo *exp.*
(Argentina) said of someone who is an extreme asshole with a great deal of nerve (or "balls") • (lit.): balled and balled.
example:
¡Armando ha intentado ligarse a mi novia! ¡Verdaderamente es un **pelotudo y un boludo**!
translation:
Armando just tried to pick up my girlfriend! He **really has nerve**!

pendejo/a *n. & adj. (Mexico)*
fucker; fucked (said of a contemptible person).
example:
¡Ese **pendejo** acaba de tirar un huevo en mi carro!
translation:
That **fucker** just threw an egg at my car!

pendejo/a de mierda *m.*
(Argentina, Mexico) an insult in reference to a trouble-making little child, "piece of shit" • (lit.): pubic hair of shit.

pendona *f.* prostitute, whore • (lit.): despicable person.

pensar que a uno lo le apesta la mierda *exp.* to think one's shit doesn't stink • (lit.): [same].

pepa *f.* vagina, "pussy" • (lit.): take from the female name "Pepa."

pepereche *m. (El Salvador)* prostitute, whore.

pepino *m.* penis, "dick" • (lit.): cucumber.

pepita *f.* clitoris • (lit.): nugget.

pera (hacerse una/la) *exp.* to masturbate, to beat off • (lit.): to make oneself a pear.

perdida *f.* prostitute • (lit.): lost.

perezoso/a *n. & adj.* lazy bum; lazy • (lit.): [same].
example:
Laura vino a mi casa para ayudarme a cocinar para la fiesta, pero yo hice casi todo el trabajo. No sabía que era tan **perezosa**.
translation:
Laura came over to my house to help me cook for our party, but I did most of the work. I didn't realize she was so **lazy**.

perico *m. (Mexico, Central and South America)* cocaine • (lit.): periwig.

periodo *m.* • (lit.): a woman's period.

pesado/a *n. & adj.* • **1.** a bore; boring • **2.** annoying • (lit.): heavy.
example -1:
El discurso de David fue **pesado**.
translation:
David's lecture was **boring**.
example -2:
Ahí está Monica. No quiero que me vea; ¡es tan **pesada**!
translation:
There's Monica. I don't want her to see me. She's so **annoying**!

pesquesuda *f.* penis, "dick."

petardo (ser un) *m.* to be a bore • (lit.): to be a torpedo, firecracker.
example:
No me gusta estar con Miguel. ¡Es tan **petardo**!
translation:
I don't like spending time with Miguel. He's such a **bore**!

petiso de mierda *m. (Argentina)* asshole, jerk • (lit.): little shit.
example:
No voy a invitar a ese **petiso de mierda** a mi fiesta de cumpleaños.
translation:
I'm not going to invite that **little shit** to my birthday party.

pezon *m.* nipple • (lit.): [same].

picha *(Cuba)* penis, "dick."
NOTE -1: **pichada** *f.* fornication, screwing.

NOTE -2: **pichar** *v.* to fornicate, to screw.

pichicato/a *n. & adj.* tightwad; stingy.
example:
¿Quieres que andemos diez millas? No seas **pichicato**. Vamos a coger un taxi.
translation:
You want us to walk ten miles? Don't be such a **cheapskate**. Let's just get a taxi.

pichicuaca *f. (El Salvador)* penis, "dick."

pichón *m.* penis, "dick" • (lit.): squab.

pichula *f. (Chile)* penis, "dick."
NOTE: This is from the verb *pichulear* meaning "to deceive."

pico *m. (Chile)* penis, "dick" • (lit.): beak.
NOTE: In some parts of South America, *y pico* is used to mean "approximately": *Te veo a las siete y pico*; I'll see you around seven o'clock.

pijo/a • **1.** *n.* penis • **2.** *adj.* snobby • *¡Qué mujer más pija!*; What a snobby woman! • **3.** *n.* stupid person.

pimiento *m.* penis, "dick" • (lit.): pimento, pepper.

pinche *n. & adj.* tightwad; stingy, cheap • (lit.): scullion, kitchen boy.
example:
Diego es un **pinche**. ¡No me invitó ni a un café el día de mi cumpleaños!

translation:
Diego is so **cheap**. He didn't even offer to buy me a cup of coffee for my birthday!

pinchón *m.* sexy girl, hot chick • (lit.): small bird.
example:
Todos los chavos en la escuela piensan que mi hermana es todo un **pichón**.
translation:
All the guys in school think my sister is a real **hot chick**.
NOTE: The masculine noun *chavo* (used in the example above) is a very popular term in Mexico meaning "guy."

pinco *m.* (*Puerto Rico*) penis, "dick" • (lit.): penis.

pinga (*Cuba, Puerto Rico*) penis, "dick" • (lit.): shoulder yoke (used for carrying).

pingo *m.* prostitute, whore.

pingona *f.* prostitute, whore.

pipí *m.* (*child's language*) urine, pee-pee.
example:
¿Has **hecho pipí** antes de irte a la cama?
translation:
Did you **go pee-pee** before going to bed?
NOTE: **hacer pipí** *exp.* to go pee-pee.

pipa *f.* • **1.** drunkard • **2.** clitoris • (lit.): pipe (for smoking tobacco).

example:
¡Qué lástima! Acabo de descubrir que la madre de Emilio es una **pipa**.
translation:
What a shame! I just found out that Emilio's mother is a **drunkard**.

pipilla *f.* clitoris.

pipote *m.* (*Southern Spain*) clitoris • (lit.): big sunflower seed.

piruja *n. & adj.* easy lay; easy • (lit.): vulgar for "slut."
example:
Elvia es una **piruja**. Ella duerme con todo el mundo.
translation:
Elvia is a **slut**. She has sex with everyone.

pirujo *m.* homosexual, "fag" • (lit.): variation of the feminine noun *piruja* meaning "an uninhibited young woman."

pirul *m.* homosexual, "fag."

pirulí *m.* penis, "dick."

pisar a *v.* to fornicate • (lit.): to step on (someone).

pisto/a *adj.* drunk, bombed • (lit.): chicken broth.
example:
Si me tomo media copa de vino, estoy **pista**.
translation:
If I drink half a glass of wine, I get **bombed**.

pistola *f.* penis, "dick" • (lit.): pistol.

pitaya *f.* vagina, "pussy" • (lit.): tropical cactus with an edible fruit.

pito *m. (Spain, Uruguay)* penis, "dick" • (lit.): horn, whistle.

pitón *m. (Puerto Rico)* vagina, "pussy" • (lit.): budding horn.

pitones *m.pl.* breasts, "tits" • (lit.): budding horns (of a bull, deer, goat, etc.).

pizarrín *m.* penis, "dick" • (lit.): slate pencil.

plátano *m.* penis, "dick" • (lit.): banana.

plantar a alguien *exp.* to dump someone • (lit.): to throw someone out.
example:
¿Has oido la noticia? Verónica **dejó plantado** a Pedro porque ¡lo agarró con otra mujer!
translation:
Did you hear the news? Veronica **dumped Pedro** because she caught him with another woman!

plomo/a *n. (Argentina)* annoying (said of a person) • (lit.): lead.
example:
Un amigo mío se queda en mi casa una semana más. Al principio no me molestaba, pero se está convirtiendo en un **plomo**.
translation:
A friend of mine is staying at my house for another week. I didn't mind at first, but he becoming more and more a **pain-in-the-ass**!

pluma *f.* prostitute • (lit.): feather.

plumero *m. (Puerto Rico)* homosexual, "fag" • (lit.): feather duster.

poca cosa *f. & adj.* runt; runty • (lit.): little thing.
example:
Mi hermana sale con un **poca cosa**. ¡Están ridículos juntos, porque ella es tan alta!
translation:
My sister is dating a **little runt**. They look ridiculous together because my sister is so tall!

polla *f. (Spain)* penis, "dick" • (lit.): young hen.

polvo (echar un) *exp.* to fornicate • (lit.): to throw a powder.

pompi(s) *m.[pl.] (children's language)* buttocks.

ponserse duro *exp.* to get an erection • (lit.): to put oneself hard.

popa *f.* buttocks • (lit.): stern (in a ship), poop-deck.

popeta *f. (Puerto Rico)* penis, "dick."

porra *f.* penis, "dick" • (lit.): club, bludgeon.

posaderas *f.* buttocks • (lit.): innkeeper.

presa fácil (ser una) *f.* to be an easy lay • (lit.): to be an easy grab.
example:
Estoy seguro de que Inés se acostará contigo; es famosa por ser **presa fácil**.

translation:
I'm sure Inés will have sex with you. She's known as **an easy lay**.

prieta *f.* penis, "dick" • (lit.): the swarthy one.

prostíbulo *m.* whorehouse (from the masculine noun *prostituto* meaning "prostitute").

puñeta (hacer) *exp.* to masturbate, to beat off • (lit.): to make a cuff.

puerco/a *n. & adj. (Argentina)* fatso • (lit.): pig.
example:
¿Te has comido la tarta entera? ¡Qué **puerco**!
translation:
You ate that entire cake? What a **pig**!

pupusa *f. (El Salvador)* vagina, "pussy" • (lit.): a tortilla filled with cheese.

purgación *f.* menstruation, period • (lit.): purging.

puta *f.* prostitute, whore.

ALSO -1: **de puta madre** *exp.* • **1.** said of something excellent • *Esa casa es de puta madre;* That house is excellent • **2.** to be in excellent shape • *Esa tipa está de puta madre;* That girl is in great shape.

ALSO -2: **ir de putas** *exp.* to walk the streets.

ALSO -3: **putada** *f.* annoyance, pain-in-the-neck.

NOTE: The term *puto/a* is commonly used in place of the adjectives *jodido/a* and *chingado/a*

both meaning "fucking": *ese jodido/chingado/puto examen;* that fucking test.

puta/o de mierda *f. (Argentina)* smelly whore • (lit.): whore of shit.

puta la madre, puta la hija *exp.* like mother, like daughter • (lit.): the mother's a whore, [so] the daughter's a whore.

puta madre *f. (Mexico)* mother fucker • (lit.): mother.
example:
¡Esa **puta madre** me acaba de dar una patada!
translation:
That **mother fucker** just kicked me!
NOTE: In Spanish, to talk about someone's mother disparagingly is a prelude to a fight.

ALSO: **me vale madre** *exp.* I don't give a fuck • (lit.): it's worth a mother to me.

puto *m. & adj.* derogatory for "homosexual," fag; faggy. • (lit.): male/female prostitute.
example:
Benito es un **puto** de gustar los hombres altos.
translation:
Benito is a **fag**. He likes tall men.
NOTE: **puta** *f. & adj.* prostitute, slut.

putonero/a *n. & adj.* from the feminine noun *puta* meaning "whore" • (lit.): one who likes whores.

example:
Ese tío es un **putonero**, siempre anda con mujerzuelas.

translation:
That guy's a real **whore-hound**. He is always hanging out with easy women.

putonga *f.* prostitute • (lit.): large prostitute, whore.

¡Qué cagada! *interj. (Argentina)* Darn! What bad luck! • (lit.): What shit!

¿Qué coño? *exp.* What the hell?
MEXICO: **¿Qué carajo?** *exp.*

¿Qué coño es esto? *exp.* What the hell is this?
MEXICO: **¿Qué carajo es esto?** *exp.*

¿Qué coño quieres? *exp.* What the hell do you want?
MEXICO: **¿Qué carajo quieres?** *exp.*

¡Qué te jodas! *interj.* Fuck off! • (lit.): May you fuck yourself!

¡Qué te la mame tu madre! *interj.* Fuck you! • (lit.): May your mother suck it for you!

quebrachón *m. (Mexico)* homosexual, "fag" • (lit.): large piece of quebracho bark.

quebracho *m. (Mexico)* homosexual, "fag" • (lit.): quebracho bark.

quedar de encargo *exp.* *(Mexico)* to make pregnant, to "knock up" • (lit.): made to order.

¿Quién coño viene? *exp.* Who the hell is coming?
MEXICO: **¿Quién carajo viene?** *exp.*

quilombo *n. (Argentina, Uruguay)* whorehouse.
NOTE: This term is commonly used in Argentina and Uruguay as an interjection: *Qué quilombo!;* What a mess!

quinto coño (estar en el) *exp.* to be somewhere very far • (lit.): to be in the fifth cunt.

quinto coño (ir al) *exp.* to go somewhere far away, to go to the boonies • (lit.): fifth cunt (to go to the).

quitarle al mondongo un peso de encima *exp. (Mexico)* to defecate • (lit.): to empty out the intestines.
example:
He desayunado tanto que tengo que **quitarle al mondongo un peso de encima**.

translation:
I ate so much breakfast that I think I need **to take a dump**.

rabo *m.* penis, "dick" • (lit.): tail.

raja *f.* vagina, "pussy" • (lit.): gash.

rajada *f.* vagina, "pussy" • (lit.): gash.

rajita *f.* vagina, "pussy" • (lit.): little slit.

ramera *f.* prostitute • (lit.): prostitute, whore.

rayado/a *n. & adj.* idiot; stupid (*Argentina*) • (lit.): striped one.
example:
Laura no sabe cómo encender su computadora. Está **rayada**.
translation:
Laura can't figure out how to turn on her computer. She's **stupid**.

reata *f.* (*Mexico*) penis, "dick" • (lit.): rope.

regarse *v.* to ejaculate, to have an orgasm • (lit.): to wet oneself.

regir *v.* (*Mexico*) to defecate • (lit.): to rule.
example:
Creo que el niño se ha **regido** otra vez en los pantalones.
translation:
I think the baby **pooped** in his pants again.

regla *f.* woman's period • (lit.): [same].

remolino del pellejo *exp.* (*Mexico*) anus • (lit.): the whirlpool of the skin.

repisas *f.pl.* (*Mexico*) breasts, "tits" • (lit.): shelves.

resbalón *m.* (*Mexico, Guatemala*) whorehouse, brothel.

retazo macizo *m.* (*Mexico*) penis, "dick" • (lit.): stiff piece.

retozona • **1.** *f.* (*Mexico*) prostitute • **2.** *adj.* frisky.

revisar los interiores *exp.* (*Mexico*) to have sex • (lit.): to check on one's insides.

revista equis *f.* dirty magazine • (lit.): an X(-rated) magazine.
example:
¡Encontré una **revista equis** en el cuarto de mi hermano pequeño! Me pregunto dónde la consiguió.
translation:
I found a **dirty magazine** in my little brother's bedroom! I wonder where he found it.

riata *f.* (*Mexico*) penis, "dick."

rifle *m.* (*Mexico*) penis, "dick" • (lit.): rifle.
NOTE: This term is borrowed from English.

rodillo *m.* penis, "dick" • (lit.): rolling pin.

romper *v.* (*Mexico*) to deflower a girl • (lit.): to tear, to break down.
VARIATION: romper el tambor *exp.* • (lit.): to bust open the screen.

rosco m. vagina, "pussy" • (lit.): ring-shaped roll of pastry.

rul m. (Mexico) anus.

rulacho m. (Mexico) anus.

rule m. (Mexico) prostitute.

ruletera f. (Mexico) prostitute.

S

sacar de quicio a alguien exp. to drive someone crazy • (lit.): to bring someone to his/her threshold (of tolerance).
example:
¡Los nuevos vecinos hacen tanto ruido! **¡Me sacan de quicio**!
translation:
The new neighbors are making so much noise! **They're driving me crazy**!

sacatón/ona n. & adj. scaredy-cat; scared • (lit.): from the verb sacar meaning "to pull away quickly."
example:
Simón no sale por la noche. Es un **sacatón**.
translation:
Simón won't go outside at night. He's a **scaredy-cat**.

sacudírsela v. to masturbate • (lit.): to shake it oneself.

safado/a n. & adj. idiot, fool; foolish • (lit.): brazen, bold.
example:
Mi nuevo jefe no deja de hablar solo. ¡Está **safado**!

translation:
My new boss keeps talking to himself all the time. He's a **real idiot**!

salame m. (Argentina) penis, "dick" • (lit.): salami.

salchicha f. penis, "dick" • (lit.): sausage.

salido/a adj. horny.
NOTE: This is a variation of the verb salir meaning "to leave."

salir con alguien exp. to date someone • (lit.): to go out with someone.
example:
Voy a **salir con** Silvia mañana por la noche. ¿Puedes recomendarme un buen restaurante?
translation:
I'm **going out with** Silvia tomorrow night. Can you suggest a good restaurant?

salir con domingo siete exp. to get prenant by accident • (lit.): to go out with the 7th of Sunday.

señorita de compañía f. prostitute • (lit.): call-girl.

seguidillas f.pl. (Mexico) diarrhea, "the runs" • (lit.): flamenco song and dance
example:
Me duele el estómago. Creo que voy a tener **seguidillas**.
translation:
My stomach hurts. I think I'm going to have **the runs**.

ser más puta que las gallinas *exp.* *(Cuba)* (said of a woman) to be as horny as a toad • (lit.): to be as slutty as the hens.

seta *f.* vagina, "pussy" • (lit.): mushroom.

sexo tribal *m.* gang bang • (lit.): tribal sex.

NOTE: This act is consensual and therefore not considered rape as is *violacion en grupo.*

SIDA *m.* AIDS • (lit.): Sindrome Inmunodeficiencia Adquirida.

singar *v.* *(Cuba)* to fornicate • (lit.): to pole or propel with an oar.

sobarse la picha *exp.* *(Costa Rica)* to masturbate • (lit.): to fondle the penis oneself.

VARIATION: **sobársela** *v.*

socotroco/a *n. & adj.* *(Cuba)* idiot; stupid.
example:
¿Por qué quieres salir con Ernesto? Es todo un **socotroco**. ¡Ni siquiera sabe cuánto son dos más dos!
translation:
Why do you want to go out with Ernesto? He's such an **idiot**. He can't even add two plus two!

¡Sola vaya! *interj.* *(Cuba)* Good riddance! • (lit.): Just go!
example:
¡No vuelvas aquí nunca! **¡Sola vaya!**
translation:
Don't ever come back here again! **Good riddance**!

sombrero de Panama *exp.* *(Mexico)* condom • (lit.): Panama's hat.

sopladores *m.pl.* *(Mexico)* testicles • (lit.): blowers, ventilators.

soplapollas *m.* *(Spain)* jackass, jerk • (lit.): cocksucker.
example:
¿Vas a salir con Pablo? ¡Es un **soplapollas**!
translation:
You're going out with Pablo? He's such a **jerk**!

soreco/a *n. & adj.* idiot; stupid *(El Salvador).*
example:
Soy tan **soreca**. No puedo descilrar cómo componer mi nueva bicicleta.
translation:
I'm so **stupid**. I just can't figure out how to assemble my new bicycle.

subir al guayabo *exp.* *(Mexico)* to have sex • (lit.): to go up to the jelly.

sunfiate *m.* *(El Salvador)* anus.

tía buena *f.* *(Spain)* hot chick • (lit.): good aunt.
example:
Tu hermana pequeña se ha convertido en una verdadera **tía buena**.

translation:
Your little sister has really turned into a **hot chick**.

NOTE: The feminine noun *tía* is commonly used in Spain to mean "woman" or "girl."

taconera *f. (Mexico)* prostitute.

NOTE: This comes from the verb *taconear* meaning "to tap one's heels."

tacuche de filiberto *m. (Mexico)* condom • (lit.): clothing of the filbert (since *filiberto* is used to mean "penis" in slang).

talonera *f.* prostitute • (lit.): someone who walks very quickly.

tamale *m.* vagina, "pussy" • (lit.): tamale.

tana *f. (Mexico)* prostitute.

tanates *m.pl. (Mexico)* testicles • (lit.): bundle, parcel.

tanta pedo para cagar aguado *exp.* much ado about nothing • (lit.): so much farting for such watery shit.

tapado/a *n. & adj.* idiot; stupid • (lit.): covered-up.
example:
Mi nueva vecina sale a la calle en bañador en pleno invierno. Creo que está un poco **tapada**.
translation:
My new neighbor wears bathing suits outside during the winter. I think she's a little **nuts**.

tarado/a *n. & adj.* idiot; stupid. • (lit.): defective, damaged.

example:
Si te crees que me voy a levantar tan pronto para llevarte al aeropuerto, ¡estás **tarado**! Vete en taxi.
translation:
If you think I'm going to get up that early to drive you to the airport, you're **nuts**! Just take a taxi.

tarugo/a *n. & adj. (Guatemala, Mexico)* idiot; stupid • (lit.): wooden peg.
example:
Creía que mi novio era normal. Pero después de unos meses me dí cuenta de que es un **tarugo**.
translation:
I thought my boyfriend was so normal. But after a few months, I realized that he's really a **crackpot**!

tecolote *m.* drunkard • (lit.): owl.
example:
Mira a ese **tecolote** de allí. ¡Creo que es mi profesor de biología!
translation:
Look at that **drunkard** over there. I think that's my biology teacher!

tener el famban barretoso *exp. (Cuba)* to have a huge butt.

tener la mecha puesta *exp. (Cuba)* to be menstruating, to be "on the rag" • (lit.): to have the fire on.

tener los mangos bajitos *exp.* (*Cuba*) to have sagging breasts • (lit.): to have low-hanging mangos.

tener una boda por todo lo alto *exp.* to have a huge wedding • (lit.): to have a wedding for all the high.
example:
Cuando me case, voy a **tener una boda por todo lo alto**.
translation:
When I get married, I'm going **to have a huge wedding**.

tener una vena *exp.* said to describe a homosexual • (lit.): to have one vein.

tenerla dura *exp.* to get an erection • (lit.): to have it hard.

tenerla tiesa *exp.* to get an erection • (lit.): to have it stiff.

teresas *f.pl.* breasts, "tits" • (lit.): Theresas.

tetas *f.pl.* breasts, "tits" • (lit.): [same].

tetona *f.* woman with large breasts (from the feminine plural noun *tetas* meaning "breasts").

tetorras *m.pl.* breasts, "tits" • (lit.): large breasts, large tits (from the feminine plural noun *tetas* meaning "breasts").

timbón/ona *n. & adj.* (*Mexico*) fatso; extremely fat.
example:
Qué vestido tan bonito, aunque estoy **timbona** para ponérmelo.
translation:
What a beautiful dress. But I'm **too fat** to fit into it.

tirar *v.* (*Peru, Ecuador, Colombia, Chile, Venezuela*) to fornicate • (lit.): to throw away.

tirarse a mamar *exp.* to give a blow job • (lit.): to pull oneself a sucking.

tirarse *v.* to fornicate • (lit.): to throw oneself.

tocársela *v.* to masturbate • (lit.): to touch it oneself.

tocar la trompeta *exp.* to give a blow job • (lit.): to play the trumpet.

tolete *m.* (*Cuba*) penis, "dick" • (lit.): club.

tomar mujer *exp.* to get married to a woman • (lit.): to take a woman.
example:
¿David ha **tomado mujer**? Creí que le gustaba ser un solterón.
translation:
David **got married**? I thought he enjoyed being a bachelor.
ALSO: **tomar hombre** *exp.* to get married to a man • (lit.): to take a man.

tompeates *m.pl.* (*Mexico*) testicles.

tonto *m.* vagina, "pussy" • (lit.): silly, foolish.

tornillo *m.* penis, "dick" • (lit.): screw.

torta *f.* (*El Salvador*) vagina, "pussy" • (lit.): cake, torte.

tortera f. lesbian, "dyke" • (lit.): tortilla maker.

tortillera f. lesbian, "dyke" • (lit.): one who sells tortillas.

tostón m. said of someone or something boring • (lit.): anything overtoasted (and therefore unwanted).
example:
Nuestro nuevo profesor de biología es un **tostón**. Me es difícil mantenerme despierto en su clase.
translation:
Our new biology teacher is such a **bore**. I have trouble staying awake in his class.

totoreco/a n. & adj. (El Salvador) idiot; stupid • (lit.): stunned, confused, bewildered.
example:
¡Quítate la pantalla de la lámpara de la cabeza! ¡La gente va a pensar que estás **totoreco**!
translation:
Take that lamp shade off your head! People are you going to think you're **crazy**!

trío m. threesome • (lit.): trio.

tragar v. to fornicate.

tranca f. (Cuba, Puerto Rico) penis, "dick" • (lit.): club, thick stick.

traque m. loud fart • (lit.): loud bang.
example:
¿Has oído ese **traque**? ¡Sonó como si alguien explotó!
translation:
Did you hear that **loud fart**? It sounded like someone exploded!

trasero m. anus • (lit.): rear.

trastero m. (Mexico) anus or asshole • (lit.): storeroom.

trasto m. penis, "dick" • (lit.): old piece of furniture, piece of lumber.

triángulo m. (Puerto Rico) homosexual, "fag" • (lit.): triangle.

trompa f. penis, "dick" • (lit.): horn.

trompudo/a n. & adj. big-mouthed person, loudmouth.
example:
Alejandro no para de hablar. Es un **trompudo**.
translation:
Alejandro never stops talking. He's such a **big-mouth**.
NOTE: This is from the feminine noun trompa meaning "elephant's trunk" or the musical instrument the "horn."

tronado/a adj. (El Salvador) drunk, bombed • (lit.): spoiled.
example:
¿Cómo te has podido beber todo el vaso de Vodka? ¡Yo estaría totalmente **tronado**!
translation:
How did you drink that entire glass of Vodka? I'd be totally **bombed**!

troncho/a n. & adj. (El Salvador) fatso; fat • (lit.): stalk, stem.

example:
Me voy a poner **troncho** como no me ponga a dieta.

translation:
I'm going to get **fat** if I don't go on a diet.

tronco m. (Puerto Rico) penis, "dick" • (lit.): trunk.

truño n. shit.
example:
Ten cuidado de no pisar un **truño**. Hay muchos perros en este barrio.

translation:
Be careful not to walk in any **shit**. There are a lot of dogs in this neighborhood.

¡Tu madre! interj. Fuck you! • (lit.): Your mother!

¡Tu madre tiene un pene! exp. Fuck you! • (lit.): Your mother has a dick!

¡Tu puta madre! interj. Fuc you! • (lit.): Your whore of a mother!

tubar v. to fornicate • (lit.): to knock down.

tunco/a n. & adj. (El Salvador) fatso; fat • (lit.): (Honduras, Mexico) hog, pig.
example:
Daniela era **tunca**, pero después de estar a régimen seis meses, está guapísima.

translation:
Daniela used to be **fat**, but after dieting for six months, she's beautiful.

un buen meneo exp. a good lay • (lit.): a good move.

un buen revolcón m. a good lay • (lit.): a good rolling about.

un vómito m. (Argentina) said of anything disgusting • (lit.): a vomit.
example:
No me voy a comer eso. ¡Parece **un vómito**!

translation:
I'm not eating that food. It looks **disgusting**!

una buena cogida f. a good lay • (lit.): a good fuck.
NOTE: This expression applies to both men and women.

una buena tranca f. a good lay • (lit.): a good thick stick.

una mierda f. (Argentina) said of something unpleasant or worthless • (lit.): a shit.

víbora f. penis, "dick" • (lit.): viper.

vaca f. fatso (applies only to a woman) • (lit.): cow.
example:
¡Este vestido me hace parecer como una **vaca**!

translation:
This dress makes me look like a **fat cow**!

vara *f.* penis, "dick" • (lit.): stick.

velga *f.* *(Puerto Rico)* penis, "dick" (from *verga* meaning "broomstick").

NOTE: In Puerto Rico, it is common to pronounce the "R" as an "L" when it occurs within a word. Even the country itself is often pronounced *Puelto Rico* by the natives.

venirse *v.* *(Mexico)* to ejaculate • (lit.): to come.

verde *f.* marijuana • (lit.): green.

veregallo *m.* *(Mexico)* masturbation.

verga *f.* • **1.** penis • **2.** stupid person ("dick-head") (lit.): broomstick.

vergallito *m.* *(Mexico)* masturbation • (lit.): small penis.

¡Vete a hacer puñetas! *exp.* *(Spain)* Fuck off! • (lit.): Go beat off!

¡Vete a joder por ahí! *interj.* Fuck off! • (lit.): Go fuck over there!

¡Vete a la [mismísima] mierda! *exp.* Go to hell! • (lit.): Go to the [very same] shit!

¡Vete a la reverenda mierda! *interj.* *(Cuba)* Go to hell! • (lit.): Go to holy shit!

¡Vete al carajo! *interj.* Go to hell! • (lit.): Go to the asshole's house!

¡Vete al coño de tu madre! *interj.* Fuck you! • (lit.): Go to your mother's cunt!

MEXICO: **¡Vete al carajo de tu madre!** *interj.*

¡Vete al diablo! *interj.* Go to hell! • (lit.): Go to the devil!

¡Vete por ahí a que te den por el culo! *interj.* Fuck you! • (lit.): Go where you'll get it up the ass!

vieja conchuda *f.* *(Argentina)* old woman • (lit.): old cunted one (from the feminine noun *concha*, literally "sea shell," used to mean "vagina" or "pussy").
example:
Nuestra profesora de matemáticas es una **vieja conchuda** que lleva enseñando miles de años.
translation:
Our math teacher is an **old relic** who's been teaching for a thousand years.

vieja tetuda *f.* *(Argentina)* old woman • (lit.): old one with tits.
example:
Espero que esa **vieja tetuda** no sea la nueva jefa.
translation:
I hope that **old lady** isn't our new boss.

viejo boludo *m.* *(Argentina)* old codger • (lit.): old one with balls.

example:
Mi médico es un **viejo boludo**, pero es buenísimo.

translation:
My doctor is an **old codger** but he's brilliant.

viejo pelotudo m. (Argentina) old codger • (lit.): old one with balls.
example:
¡No me puedo creer que dejen a un **viejo pelotudo** como ese detrás del volante!

translation:
I can't believe that they let an **old codger** like that behind the wheel!

viejo rabo verde m. dirty old man • (lit.): old green tail.
example:
¡Ese hombre está saliendo con una mujer veinte años más joven que él! Yo creo que es un **viejo rabo verde**.

translation:
That man is dating a girl twenty years younger than he is! I think he's just a **dirty old man**.

viejo/a de mierda n. "old fart" • (lit.): old person of shit.

violación en grupo f. gang bang • (lit.): group violation.

NOTE: This act is nonconsensual and considered rape as opposed to *sexo tribal*.

volteado m. homosexual, "fag" • (lit.): turned around.

volver loco/a a alguien exp. to drive someone crazy • (lit.): to turn someone crazy.

example:
El tráfico de esta ciudad me está **volviendo loco**.

translation:
All the traffic in this city is **making me crazy**.

vomitar hasta la primera papilla exp. to vomit, to barf one's guts up • (lit.): to vomit even one's first soft-food.
example:
Estuve tan enfermo la semana pasada, que **vomité hasta la primera papilla**.

translation:
I was so sick last week that **I barfed my guts up**.

vomitar hasta las tripas exp. to vomit, to barf one's guts up • (lit.): to vomit up to one's guts.
example:
Creo que anoche me sentó algo mal. Estuve **vomitando hasta las tripas** durante tres horas.

translation:
I think I had food poisoning last night. I was **vomiting my guts up** for three hours.

¡Y una mierda! exp. Bullshit! • (lit.): And a shit!

yiyi m. (Puerto Rico) homosexual, "fag."

yoyo *m.* *(Mexico)* vagina, "pussy."

yuca *f.* *(El Salvador)* penis, "dick" • (lit.): yucca plant.

Z

zacate inglés *m.* *(Mexico and Central America)* marijuana • (lit.): English hay.

zanahoria *f.* penis, "dick" • (lit.): carrot.

zapato *m.* *(Argentina)* idiot, jerk • (lit.): shoe.
example:
¿Has visto el sombrero que lleva Miguel? ¡Parece un **zapato**!
translation:
Did you see the hat Miguel is wearing? It makes him look like a **jerk**!

zonas (las) *f.pl.* red light districts in Mexico and Colombia • (lit.): areas (the).

zoofilia *m.* bestiality.

zopenco/a *n. & adj.* jerk; stupid • (lit.): dull, stupid.
example:
¡Nunca saldría con Jorge! ¡Es un **zopenco**!

translation:
I'd never go out with Jorge! He's such a **jerk**!

zorra *f.* bitch • (lit.): fox.
example:
¿Has conocido ya a la nueva jefa? ¡Es una **zorra**!
translation:
Did you meet the new boss? She's such a **bitch**!

zullarse *v.* to fart • (lit.): to fart.
example:
La próxima vez que tengas que **zullarte**, por favor levántate de la mesa.
translation:
The next time you have **to fart**, please leave the table.

zullón *m.* fart • (lit.): fart.
example:
¡Hay un **zullón** que ha estado pululando por esta habitación durante una hora!
translation:
There's a **fart** that's been lingering in this room for an hour!

zurrar *v.* to defecate • (lit.): to reprimand, to hit.
example:
Si tienes que **zurrar**, usa el otro baño. Este está roto.
translation:
If you need **to take a dump**, use the other toilet. This one isn't working.

NOTE -1: In Argentina, this verb means "to fart silently."

NOTE -2: **zurullo/zurullón** m. turd • (lit.): hard lump.

zurullo m. turd • (lit.): hard lump.
example:
Cuidado donde juegas. Hay muchos **zurullos** en este parque.

translation:
Be careful where you play. There are **turds** all over this park.

zurullón m. turd • (lit.): hard lump.
example:
¡Ah, no! ¡He pisado un **zurullón** y he estropeado mis zapatos nuevos!

translation:
Oh, no! I stepped in a **turd** and ruined my new shoes!

Caslon Books

——— ORDER FORM ON BACK ———

Prices subject to change

SPANISH	BOOK	CASSETTE
STREET SPANISH 1 . . . . *The Best of Spanish Slang*	$15.95	$12.50
STREET SPANISH 2 . . . . *The Best of Spanish Idioms (available '98)*	$15.95	$12.50
STREET SPANISH 3 . . . . *The Best of Naughty Spanish (available '98)*	$15.95	$12.50
STREET SPANISH SLANG DICTIONARY . . . . *(available '98)*	$16.95	

FRENCH	BOOK	CASSETTE
STREET FRENCH 1 . . . . *The Best of French Slang*	$15.95	$12.50
STREET FRENCH 2 . . . . *The Best of French Idioms*	$15.95	$12.50
STREET FRENCH 3 . . . . *The Best of Naughty French*	$15.95	$12.50
STREET FRENCH SLANG DICTIONARY & THESAURUS	$16.95	

AMERICAN-ENGLISH	BOOK	CASSETTE
STREET TALK 1 . . . . *How to Speak & Understand American Slang*	$16.95	$12.50
STREET TALK 2 . . . . *Slang Used in Popular American TV Shows*	$16.95	$12.50
STREET TALK 3 . . . . *The Best of American Idioms*	$18.95	$12.50
BIZ TALK 1 . . . . *American Business Slang & Jargon*	$16.95	$12.50
BIZ TALK 2 . . . . *More American Business Slang & Jargon*	$16.95	$12.50
BLEEP! . . . . *A Guide to Popular American Obscenities*	$14.95	$12.50

GERMAN	BOOK	CASSETTE
STREET GERMAN 1 . . . . *The Best of German Idioms*	$16.95	$12.50

Caslon Books

P.O. Box 519 • Fulton, CA 95439 • USA

TOLL FREE Telephone/FAX (US/Canada):
1-888-4-ESLBOOKS (1-888-437-5266)

International orders Telephone/FAX line:
707-546-8878

ORDER FORM

Name _____

(School/Company) _____

Street Address _____

City _____ State/Province _____ Postal Code _____

Country _____ Phone _____

Quantity	Title	Book or Cassette?	Price Each	Total Price

Total for Merchandise	
Sales Tax (California Residents Only)	
Shipping (See Below)	
ORDER TOTAL	

METHOD OF PAYMENT (check one)

☐ Check or Money Order   ☐ VISA   ☐ Master Card   ☐ Discover
(Money orders and personal checks must be in U.S. funds and drawn on a U.S. bank.)

Credit Card Number: Card Expires:

☐☐☐☐ ☐☐☐☐ ☐☐☐☐ ☐☐☐☐ ☐☐☐☐ ☐☐☐☐   ☐☐ ☐☐

Signature *(important!)* ➜

SHIPPING

Domestic Orders: SURFACE MAIL (delivery time 5-7 days).
Add $4 shipping/handling for the first item · $1 for each additional item.
RUSH SERVICE available at extra charge.

International Orders: OVERSEAS SURFACE (delivery time 6-8 weeks).
Add $5 shipping/handling for the first item · $2 for each additional item.
OVERSEAS AIRMAIL available at extra charge.